TOBACCO AND SMOKING

Dr. Amit Krishna De

Ph.D, FICN, FNESA, FAEB, FIABS

BOOKS FOR ALL

Delhi-110052

Distributed By:
D K Publishers Distributors P Ltd.
1, Ansari Road, Darya Ganj,
New Delhi-110002
Phones: 3261465, 3278368
Fax No: 3264368
e-mail: dkpd@del3.vsnl.net.in
visit us at: www.dkpdindia.com

First Published 2000

ISBN 81-7386-219-2

Published By:
BOOKS FOR ALL
B-2, Vardhaman Palace,
Nimri Commercial Centre,
Ashok Vihar Phase-IV
Delhi-110052
Phone: 7401672, 7452453
e-mail: lpp@nde.vsnl.net.in
visit us at: www.lppindia.com

Printed At:
D K Fine Art Press P Ltd.
Delhi-110052

PRINTED IN INDIA

Contents

Dedicated To

MR. SAMIR KUMAR DAS
&
MRS. KRISHNA DAS

Foreword

Dr. Amit Krishna De, a very young and prolific science writer has written a new book entitled " Tobacco and Smoking". It is indeed a new book on an old subject. In my opinion, the book will be a provocative one and expected to raise a debate, scientific and cultural. Dr. De has begun from the beginning. He has given a good account of the agrobotany of the tobacco plant- the main concern of the book. Dr. De has lucidly portrayed the nature of the nicotine in the tobacco plant from biochemical viewpoint.

Nicotine like Quinine is an important alkaloid. Almost all alkaloids are poisons if used beyond the threshold limit and almost all poisons are used as medicine, of course the dose must be proper. He has also highlighted the history of smoking which is really very interesting. Smoking in one form or other is a kind of aristocracy and at the time it is a kind of addiction.

"Cigarette smoking is injurious to health"- a statutory warning call is now well publicized. Nobody cared to bother about smoking until and unless it has found to be linked up with cancer. Now many people all over the world are scared of smoking. Who is not afraid of cancer? However all the aspects of smoking from benefits to losses are nicely depicted in the book. As Dr. De is a competent biochemist, he could discuss the problem in a scientific manner. He has also given some news from research world which I believe would be news to many. I hope this popular and provocative book will be useful to understand the aftermath of smoking, and I also hope,smokers, non-smokers and doctors and social workers will greatly appreciate this book.

Prof. Naresh Chandra Datta, M.Sc, Ph.D. FNESA.

Dept. of Zoology, Calcutta University & Chairman,
National Environmental Science Academy,
West Bengal Chapter.

Preface

Tobacco, initially used because of its medicinal properties, is now a menance to the society. Different forms of tobacco consumed by human beings cause not only harm to human health but also moral deterioration. The effects are more prominent for the smokers as well as for the passive smokers also. The decrease of morality through different forms of cancer is the responsibility of smoke, specially tobacco smoke.

Tobacco, initially used because of its medicinal properties, is now a menance to the society. Different form of tobacco consumed by human beings cause not only harm to human health but also moral deterioration. The effects are more prominent for the smokers as well as for the passive smokers also. The decrease of morality through different forms of cancer is the responsibility of smoke, specially tobacco smoke.

Environment includes not only air, water or soil but also refers to the one created by cultural habits of individuals. Women and children are more susceptible to the ill effects of smoking. Chewing tobacco causes oral cancer. Hence, tobacco should be totally banned. It is not only the responsibility of the government to prohibit smoking but it is also the responsibility of the individuals to stop smoking and prevent others from smoking and using tobacco products. Until and unless, the society is made aware of the ill effects of smoking, there will not be total abolishment of tobacco uses.

This book on "Tobacco and Smoking" has been written with the objective of making the society become aware of the health hazards of tobacco products particularly cigarette smoking. The different constituents of smoke and their effects on human health will reveal how smoking can act as a slow poison. In this respect, stress have been given on nicotine which is the most harmful compound in tobacco leaf. A little botanical and agricultural aspects of the plant has also been discussed to make people know more about this plant.

A comparative evaluation has been given on the effects of smoking in different parts of the world and on children, adolescence, aged and women. Steps have been suggested for reducing smoking at both government and individual levels. Some concrete suggestions have been made to help individuals in quitting smoking. The research news from all over the world at the end of the book will help the individual to know about the current research developments in the area of tobacco products and their effects on human health. I hope that this book will discourage individuals from smoking and encourage them to quit smoking and use of tobacco products.

This book will be helpful to all environmentalist, biologists, biochemists, social reformers, health club members, clinicians and researchers on the above area. This book will be a valuable asset to all the libraries, whether institutional or individual and to all the parents, who want to protect their children from the devasting effects of smoking.

Amit Krishna De

TOBACCO

"Tobacco, an outlandish weed
Doth in the land strange wonders weed,
It faints the breath, the blood it dries,
It burns the head, it blinds the eyes,
It dries the lungs, scourgeth the lights,
It nubs the soul, it dulls the sprites,
It brings a man into maze,
and make him sit for other"s gaze,
It mars a man, it mars a purse,
A lean one fat, a fat one worse,
a white man black, a black man white,
a night a day, a day a night,
It turns the brain like cat in pan
and makes a jack or Gentleman."

- Fiarholt

CHAPTER I
TOBACCO

1.1 History of Tobacco

Tobacco is considered the "golden leaf of India", just like jute is considered the "golden fibre of Bengal". In India tobacco is said to have been introduced by the Portuguese in the beginning of the seventeenth century. Its cultivation now extends to all parts of the country. It is said that a Spanish physician sent to Mexico first introduced the plant to Europe in 1560. About this time, Jean Nicot, the French Ambassador in Portugal learnt of tobacco in Lisbon and introduced it to the French Court. He promised its cultivation in the belief that it has medicinal values. The botanical name of the plant, " Nicotiana" and the word nicotine are derived from his name.

Although humans probably began sampling tobacco during the first millennium, based on the Mayan stone carvings dated about AD 600 to 900, physicians did not begin to suspect in earnest that the plant could produce ill effects until around the 19th century. The renowned Colonial physician Benjamin Rush condemned tobacco in his writings as early as 1798. Crewman who accompanied Columbus to the new world was the first European to observe the smoking of tobacco. In the following century, nicotine was isolated from tobacco leaves and was used as a drug in therapeutic fields but despite vigorous official oppositions and penalties, the use of tobacco leafs for consumption of smoking spread throughout the world rapidly.

1.2 Morphology of Tobacco Plant

Out of 60 species, the species of Nicotiana under cultivation as tobacco are *N. tabacum* Linn. and *N. rustica* Linn. (Sundararaj and Thulasidas, 1993). The original habitat of the genus is considered to be South America, particularly regions surrounding the *Andes*.

(i) *N. tabacum* linn: stout annual, about three meters high with a thick erect stem producing a few branches; leaves decurrent ovate, elliptic or lanceolate, apex acuminate, petiole winged and with a frilled auricle clasping the stem; inflorescence panicle, distinct; flowers pedicillate and permaphrodite, sepals five forming a calyx tube; corolla tube 10 to 15 mm long and 2 to 3 mm wide, lower half cylindric, pale green or creamy, upper half similar in colour or pink to red, expanded into deep cup, stamens inserted on base of corolla throat, erect with four stamens of one length, the fifth being shorter, ovary superior, bicarpellary, axile placentation, ovules numerous; style slender, stigma capitate; capsule narrow, elliptic, avoid or obricular, acute or blunt 15 to 18 mm; seeds numerous and minute. The usual seed rate adopted is 3 kg/hectare or nursery which can supply seedings for 100 to 150 hectares.

(ii) *N. rustica* linn. : Annual, reaching a height of about a metre or a little more; stem and slender branches pubescent; leaves about 30 cm. long and 20 cm. broad, oval elliptic, cordate, lanceolate or subrotund with unequal base; the distince petiole is often shorter than the blade; panicles short and compacted into a thyrse; calyx cylindric, pubescent, membranous and narrow with pointed sepals, with a longer odd sepal; corolla greenish yellow, 1.2 to 1.5 cm long, pubescent with tube proper about 3 mm long and 2 mm wide; stamens five with four of them logn and one short, ovary superior, bicarpellary; capsule elliptic, oviod or subglobose, 7 to 15 mm. This plant requires a cooler climate and its cultivation is confined mainly to the Northern and North Eastern areas of India i.e. Punjab, U.P., West Bengal, Bihar, Assam.

1.3 Commercial Types of Tobacco

1. **Cigarette or Flue Cured Tobacco:** *N. tabacum:* These are considered to have been derived from Virginia Orinoco. This variety has widely space leaves on the stalk. The promising varieties in virginia are Harrison special, Chatham, Delcrest and Virginia Gold. They are grown mostly in Andhra Pradesh.

2. **Bidi Tobacco:** *N. tabacum:* This is mainly grown in Gujarat, Maharashtra and in Nipani in Mysore. The important varieties are Kehu, Piliu and Gandiu. The leaves of these varieties are generally twelve to thirteen inches long

and five to nine inches broad, thick in texture, strong in flavour and green to yellowish brown in colour. The varieties Mirji, Nipani, Sanghi and Janavari are grown in Nipani. *N. rustica:* Pandharpuri, a variety of this species is grown in the Nipani area. It is used for giving strength to bidi mixtures.

3. **Cigar and Cheroot types:** These types are mostly grown in Tamil Nadu and in West Bengal. The Cigar leaf is brown to dark brown in colour, thin in texture and mild to medium and even strong in flavour. Its length varies from 45 to 60 cm. and breadth from 10 to 22.5 cm. The colours of the cured leaves produced in Tamil Nadu and used in cheroots is dark brown to almost black. The bhengi variety of Jati tobacco grown in West Bengal and used in manufacture of cheroots is greenish brown in colour, medium in texture and strength. In Tamil Nadu, the chief varieties are Vellavazhai, Karuzhai, Karingkappal and Oosikappal. In Andhra Pradesh, Lanka of Godavari, Natu and Chebrolu of Guntur, Japalam and Surukatti of Visakhapatnam and Desavali of West Godavari are important.

4. **Hookah types:** Both *N. tabacum* and *N. rustica* are used for Hookah. N. tabacum: The leaf is greenish brown, thin to medium is texture and moderately strong. Hookah tobacco grown in West Bengal and Assam is called Jati, Desi in Bihar and Poorbi in U.P. *N. rustica:* It is mostly grown in Punjab and Uttar Pradesh. The cured leaf is medium to thick, coarse in texture, greenish brown and strong and pungent in flavour. The improtant varities are Calcutta, Motihari and Vilayati. Motihari, grown in northern area of West Bengal, is the strongest Hookah tobacco.

5. **Chewing and Snuff types:** *N. tabacum*. These types are cultivated in Tamil Nadu, Bihar, Assam, U.P. and West Bengal. The leaf is medium to thick in texture and has a pungent aroma. The important chewing varieties in other states are Desi and Jati. Kalichopadia and Judi tobacco of Gujarat are also largely used for chewing and snuff. Important chewing varieties in Tamil Nadu and Monna (Madurai and Coimbatore districts.), Vazhaikappal (Coimbatore dists.), Periavadamugam (Madurai and Coimbatore dists.), Sivapuri (South Aracot dist.), and Vedaranayam selections (Thanjavur dist.) *N. rustica:* Leaves of Motihar grown in West Bengal, Vilayati in Assam and Calcuttia in Punjab and U.P. are also used for chewing and snuff.

6. **Wrapper Types:** It is mainly cultivated in West Bengal. Large scale cultivation was started after the partition of Bengal mainly to meet the internal requirements. Dixie shade is the popular strain.

1.4 Cultivation

Tobacco crop requires temperature of 21 to 32°C during its growth. Though tobacco trives best in tropical regions with warm climates it is also grown in temperate regions during the warmer part of the year. During very hot weather and high temperatures there is loss of moisture from the tissues of the growing plant and as a result the leaves become thicker and the aroma becomes stronger. High wind seriously affect the normal growth of the plants and also the quality of the leaves. Atmosperic humidity which has a direct relationship with the plant and the soil moisture, influence the quality of the leaf and also the yield.

Tobacco grows best on sandy loam surface soil and a slightly finer sub-soil having ample internal drainage, good aeration and high moisture holding capacity. The mineral content of the soil plays an important role in the growth of the plant. Effects of some of the important minerals are given below:

(i) **Nitrogen:** Under field conditions a range of 2 to 5% of nitrogen in leaf and 2 to 4% in stalk has been reported. Nitrogen has the most profound effect on the growth of the plants and the quality of the leaf produced. It is a constituent of the protoplasm chlorophyll, nicotine and other important substances present in the plant. With excess of nitrogen supply, the carbohydrate-nitrogen ratio gets reduced. It is observed from field trails, that in chewing, bidi and hookah tobaccos better quality is generally associated with higher yields that my be obtained from an abudant supply of nitrogen together with other nutrients. But in flue cured tobacco better quality leaves are obtained from partially nitrogen starved plants.

When nitrogen supply is low, the nitrogen content of the leaf falls below 1.5 to 2.0% . Shortage in nitrogen results in low water content in the plant, delayed flowering, low nicotine content and reduced size of the leaves.

(ii) **Phosphorus:** This is an essential constituent of protoplasm and is assimilated into protein, lecithin and other products. It plays an important role in the growth and development of the plants. A normal tobacco plant contains 0.62 g. of phosphorus. Symptoms caused by the deficiency of phosphorus have not so far being observed under the field condition in India. When there is shortage, plants assume a rosette condition, producing narrower and smaller leaves of a dark green colour. The rate of growth is slowed down and maturity is delayed.

(iii) **Potassium:** Potash is important for normal, healthy growth, and also produces drought resistance. A good supply increases the leaf area, turgor and water-holding capacity of the leaf, thus imparting a smoothness to leaf free from drought spots. Potash content is associated with good quality in most commercial varieties of tobacco. A liberal supply imparts a good burning capacity of combustibility to smoking tobaccos. Deficiency symptoms appear first in the lower leaves as chlorosis at the tips and margins, and later show dead areas here and there. In course of time the upper leaves also develop this type of symptom. Because of this the quality gets seriously affected with regard to the physical charateristics of the leaf which then burn very poorly.

(iv) **Calcium:** The calcium requirements of the tobacco plant is high. It is present in the cells as oxalates. The normal range of Calcium in leaf is 3 to 7%. An excess supply of calcium favours vegetative growth and delays leaf maturity. This neutralizes the toxic effect of magnesium and manganese. Unlike most other elements calcium does not get translocated from the lower to the top leaves and the growing regions as in other cases. Hence a constant supply of calcium must be assured throughout the life cycle to prevent deficiency. In extreme cases of calcium deficiency, chlorosis appears and the yield and quality of the plants are greatly impaired. The leaves show malformation and thickening.

(v) **Magnesium:** Magnesium constitutes about 2% of chlorophyll and therefore plays a vital part is photosynthesis. It is found to have an inverse relationship with calcium and pottasium. The tobacco plant contains 0.81% of MgO S and drown occurs in the leaf due to its deficiency. The quality is affected badly as the leaf lacks weight, body, colour and elasticity. The ash will be dark in colour.

(vi) **Sulphur:** Sulphur is a constituent of amino acids and certain proteins. The sulphur content of the plant is 0.37% of dry matter. Under deficiency conditions a plant as a whole becomes light yellow in colour and this is more prevalent in the upper leaves. In cases of severe deficiency the tips of young leaves curl downwards.

(vii) **Iron:** Iron is essential from the nutritional point of view. Under deficiency conditions interveinal chlorosis of the young leaves in the terminal bud occurs.

(viii) **Manganese:** The maganese content varies form 0.05% to 0.2% of the dry matter in the leaf. The deficiency occurs more in alkaline soil owing to its non-availability in such soils. The symptoms first appear in the young leaves as interveinal chlorosis followed by extensive necrotic spotting. In excess, the plants manifest toxic effects which appear as chlorosis followed by spotting. The cured leaf shows a dark muddy appearance.

(ix) **Boron:** The deficiency symptoms are similar to those of calcium deficiency. In cases of severe deficiency the terminal bud dies. The lower leaves become enlarged and thickened as in topped plants. In excess amounts the plants amount stunted.

(x) **Copper:** Copper is required only in traces. In cases of deficiency, the younger leaves lose their turger and show permanent wilting.

(xi) **Chlorine:** A normal plant contains 0.89% chlorine. A moderate quantity improves the yield and quality of tobacco. In Excess amounts if affects carbohydrate metabolism. The burning quality of the leaf is said to be impaired when chlorine content runs to about 1% or more.

1.5 Quality Characteristics of Tobacco Leaves

Colour is an important characteristic of tobacco which indicates the strength, the darker the colour, the stronger is the tobacco. Virginia tobacco from cigarettes have generally light colour: the best leaf being of bright lemon colour. For cigar wrappers the leaf should be large, light brown and thin. For cherrots darker coloured leaves are also used. For chewing, tobacco of a dark colour gives a pungent taste. For snuff, tobacco leaves of a reddish colour are preferred. Texture is associated with the leaf blade and the veins which form the left webs. The thicker the leaf, the greater its strength or nicotine content. As thin and silky leaf is the best for cigarettes. For cheroots, the wrapper leaf should be thin, smooth, glossy, pilable and free from prominent veins. For "Filters" or the inner contents of a cigar or cheroot, the leaf may be thick or medium. For bidis, a thick but not coarse leaf, broken into bits is preferred. For chewing tobacco, the leaf is of variable thickness, very thick and coarse leaves being considered usually inferior.

The size of leaf is very important for chewing and cheroot tobaccos. Larger leaves being preferred. For wrapper of cigar and cheroot also large leaves are preferred. For the cigarette types as virginia all sizes above 15cm are used.

Strength refers to the mildness of the pungency of the cured leaf which is dependent upon the nicotine content. As already seen under colour, the strength is often related to the colour. The following are the average nicotine contents of cured leaves used for various purposes (Sundararaj & Thulasidas, 1993).

1. For cigarettes 1.2 to 3 %. For superior cigarettes milder or neutral strengths are used.

2. For cigars bild brands 0.5 to 1.5 %. Pipe tobacco is also of the mild type: strong brands 2.25 to 3.25 %.

3. For cheroots upto 5.25 %.

4. For bidis 2.5 to 5.5 %.

5. For hookah 3.00 to 7.00 %.

6. For chewing 2.50 to 5.50 %.

The leaf used for any smoking purposes should burn slowly with regular and continous burning. The colour of the smoke is another character looked for.

The content of the ash and the colour of the ash left is another important character. White ash is preferred.

for cigarettes	-	-	-	ash left upto 1 %
Cigar	-	-	-	16 to 221/2 %
Bidi	-	-	-	19 %
Hookah	-	-	-	upto 25 %

The aroma or flavour is characteristics of the variety and also within each variety according to the cultural and curing conditions. Damaged leaves, diseased patches or spongy leaves are not preferred in the market for cigarettes, cigar or cheroot manufacture.

1.6 Nicotine Content

Tobacco leaves contain nicotine, an alkaloid that is the active principle of the plant (for details see section 2.3). The following are a few of the important points which have been put forward by the various research workers on the crop.

1. Nicotine content is genetically controlled; varieties are inherently different in their nicotine content.

2. Disease-resistant varieties are lower in nicotine content than the non-resistant varieties.

3. Nicotine accumulation is directly related to the level of nitrogen fertility.

4. After topping and desuckering, nicotine is concentrated in the remaing tissues. The degree of concentration is related to the completeness of topping and desuckering.

5. Irrigation have shown that moisture supply is the most important factor affecting nicotine.

While the above factors affect the nicotine content in tobacco, it has also been found that the following have little or no effect on nicotine: (a) closer spacing; (b) manuring with phosphorus, pottasium, calcium, chlorine and sulphur; (c) minor plant foods as boron, copper, zinc and molybdenum; and (d) fumingants like dichloropropane, ethylene dibromide.

It has also been pointed out that nicotine is produced in the roots of the tobacco plant from simple compounds made in the leaves plus nitrogen from the soil. Once nicotine is formed in the roots, it is said to be carried to the leaves and stem where it accumulates. Of all the plant foods only the nitrogen increasing applications were directly and significantly accompained by increased nicotine concentrations in the cured tobacco. With the same amount of nitrogen supply per plant, the spacing does not affect the nicotine content but when there is competition for the nitrogen supply in the field due to increased number of plants nicotine content is affected.

1.7 Uses of Tobacco

Tobacco is used largely as a "fumitory" and also as a mesticatory. For snuff, the cured leaves are freed from the stalk and thick veins, cut into pieces, fried and powdered. Then the powder is ground into very fine powder with lime and ghee passed through the fine cloth or silk sieves. Scented snuff is prepared by addition of musk, boric acid, ammonium salts, after of roses, etc. in varying portions.

The stems, the petioles, the midribs and the waste accumulates obtained during manufacture of products are used for the extraction of nicotine. Nicotine is in demand as an insecticide used in the control of parasites in cattle, sheep and poultry. After extraction of the nicotine, the residue is needed as a condition for the fertilizer mixtures with low nitrogen and high potash.

The seeds of tobacco though very small contain 30 to 40% oil. A normal plant may produce upto 400 capsules yielding over 20 gms. of seeds. A hectare may produce 125 to 140 kg of seeds. The oil obtained from the seeds is a semi-drying oil and is edible. The oil is free from nicotine, it is also used for burning and for soap making. Because of its semi-dry nature, it is also used as a substitute for linseed oil for special paints, varnishes and enamel.

After the extraction of the oil, the seed cake has 3.5% nitrogen and can be used as organic manure. The cake has been found to have no deleteriuos effect as cattle feed.

Recently, the protein extracted from tobacco leaves have been used for human consumption as it is found to be better than egg white, cheese or milk (New Scientist, **126** (1720), 29, 1990). The fibrous residue left after the extraction of the protein would also make safer cigarettes than ordinary tobacco, because burning protein generates nitrogen dioxide, cyanides and carcinogens. The "fraction one" protein comes from chloroplasts. This protein has a more balanced mixture of essential amino acids than many other foods. With high intensive cultivation, an acre of tobacco can yield over 200 kilograms of the tasteless, odourless, protein. Processing also yields other soluble protein, fibres and a mixture of starch and insoluble protein plus a liquid residue that represents most of the original biomass. Nicotine ends up in the liquid which can be used as fertiliser as the nicotine is toxic to the insects. The leaf protein will also be available to help to meet the rising food needs of developing countries, many of which have limited agricultural lands.

CHAPTER 2
SMOKING

"Thou in such a cloud dost bind us
That our worst foes cannot find us,
And ill fortune, that would thwart us,
Shoots at rovers, shooting at us;
While each man, through thy heightening steam,
Does like a smoking Etna seem."

Charles Lamb

2.1 History of Smoking

Nicotine was first isolated from the leaves of the tobacco plant by Posselt and Reiman in 1828. By the mid to late 1800s, many prominent physicians were expressing concern about the development of certain medical problems connected with tobacco. They suggested a relation between smoking and coronary artery diseases, even recognizing the potential association between passive smoking (inhaling smoke from the air) and heart problem. They also noted a correlation with lip and nasal cancer.

Although tobacco use was relatively common in that century, it did not produce the widespread illnesses it does today. Individuals of the time consumed only small amounts, mostly in the form of pipe tobacco, cigars, chewing tobacco or snuff. Cigarette smoking was rare. Then, in 1881, came the invention of the cigarette-rolling machine, followed by the development of safety matches. Both significantly encouraged smoking. In the mid-nineteenth century, new varieties of tobacco, changes in the technology of curing the leaf and machinery for mass production facilitated the spread of a new product-the cigarette-cheaper and neater than cigars and yielding a smoke so mild that it could be inhaled. By 1945 cigarettes had largely replaced other forms of tobacco consumption. Smokers increased their average of 40 cigarettes a year in 1880 to an averages of 12,854 cigarettes in 1980, the peak of American consumption per individual smoker.

The rise of tobacco use made the adverse effects of smoking more apparent. Medical reports in the 1920s strengthened the suspected links between tobacco and cancers. The connection to life span was first noted in 1939, when an article in the journal "Science" suggested that heavy smokers had a shorter life expectancy than non smokers.

In 1964 US Surgeon General Luther Terry released a truly landmark public health document. The work of an independent body of scientists, it was the country's first widely publicized official recognition that smoking causes cancer and other diseases. In many subsequent reports by the Surgeon General's office, cigarette smoking has been identified as the leading source of preventable morbidity and premature morality in the US.These statements enumerate many experimental studies in which animals have been exposed to tars, gases and other constituents in tobacco and tobacco smoke.

2.2 Constituents of Smoke

Whats in a smoke? The answer is "plenty". The smoke produced by burning a cigarette or bidi of cigar or cherrot has hundreds of chemicals some of which have been identified as highly toxic.

Cigarette smoking is technically defined as a "Heterogeneous" aerosol produced by incomplete combustion of tobacco leaf (Wilson *et al*, 1991). To be lucid, cigarette smoke is a mixture of hot air and gases that suspend various tiny particles, collectively called "Tar". Both these tars and gaseous components of the smoke are hazardous to human health. Cigarette smoke is an aerosol having a discontinous phase (about 8% by weight) and a continous phase (about 19% by weight) composed of vapor phase constituents, the rest (about 58%) representing gaseous compounds (Keith and Tesh,1965).

About 400 compounds are generated from the burning of tobacco, the smoke can be separated into gaseous and praticulate phases. The composition of the actual smoke delivered to the smoker depends not only on the composition of the tobacco but also on how densely it is packed, the length of the column of the tobacco and the temperature at which the tobacco is burnt. Rapid drawing of smoke raises the temperature of the burning tip and changes the size of the particles and the composition of both the gaseous and particluate phases. These changes may in term alter what is trapped in the filter. It is possible to specify the amount of nicotine, tar and carbon monoxide delivered by a given cigarette when it is smoked by a machine under constant condition in experimental laboratories.

(a) **Tar:** Fingers of smokers are usually discoloured by ugly brown stains. Similar stains can also be seen if you open the filter of a used cigarette or while cleaning a cigarette's filter. The substance which causes these stains is tar. Tar also stains teeth and lungs. It is unpleasant brownish black stick mixture of chemicals in which hundreds of different substances have been identified. Many of these are carcinogens or substances capable of producing cancer. Tar is what remains after the moisture and nicotine are subtracted and consists primarily of polycyclin aromatic hydrocarbons.

In 1987, two American scientists, D.E.Dusek and D.A. Girdano have reported that a few of the tar particles of cigarette smoke are definitely carcinogens, substances that can cause cancer. Polycyclic aromatic hydrocarbons are potent carcinogens. Among these are nonvolatile nitosoamines and aromatic amines, which play a major role in causing blood cancer. One such compound, benzopyrene, is among the most potent carcinogens knows so far. Also contained in the tars are phenolic compounds, which are known to speed up or activate dormant cancer cells (Dusek and Girdano, 1987). These two scientists have also reported that the smoking of a single cigarette releases into the, air surrounding the smoker, approximately 70mg of tars. Those who are smokers, can now calculate the amount of tars that they discharge into the air breathed in by others, in a day, in a month and in a year.

It is not yet sharply known how many compounds of cigarette smoke are significantly hazardous for the sidestream or passive smokers, but there is not doubt that at least, some are quiet harmful. Cigarette smoke contains at least 1,200 different toxic chemicals of which appears to be a potent source of environmental carcinogens (Table-1).

Table: I

Important constituents of cigarette smoke

Substance	Property
Particulate phase	
Polycyclic aromatic hydrocarbons	Carcinogens (cancer initiaters & pro moters)
Dibenzacridines dibenzocarbazolers and azarenes	Cancer initiators
Methyl indoles, methyl carbazoles and catechols	Co-carcinogens
Aromatic amines	Bladder carcinogens
Nicotine & other alkaloids	Toxins co-carcinogens & Irritants
Phenols	Cancer promoters
Gaseous phase	
Nitrosamines, hydrazines, vinyl chlorides, Urethane, pyridines, aldehydes (formaldeyhde, acetaldehyde, acroline), hydrogen cyanide, nitrogen oxides.	Carcinogens

(Balasubramanium 1982)

(b) **Carbon monoxide**- Cigarette smoke contains about 5 % carbon monoxide (a deadly poisonous gas). There is evidence that the so-called "safer" filter cigarettes produce an even higher percentage of carbon monoxide, because air is not drawn through the side of the filter, and the combustion is even less complete than in untrapped cigarettes.

The amount of carbon monoxide in a cigarette is certainly not sufficient to kill the smoker but it is a slow poison. When carbon monoxide enters the bloodstream it combines with the redcolouring matter of the blood (haemoglobin). Normally haemoglobin carries the vital supply of oxygen to the cells, but it combines more readily with carbon monoxide than the oxygen. In case of a lethal dose, the haemoglobin becomes saturated with carbon monoxide and death result because the system becomes completely starved of oxygen. However, in case of a heavy smoker as much as 15% of haemoglobin may be carrying carbon monoxide instead of oxygen. The result is that the oxygen supply to the whole system and particularly to the heart is severely reduced. The heart in turn is forced to work harder to pump the oxygen that is available. Doctors suspects that this may be another major factor in the development of coronary heart diseases.

Carbon monoxide, produced by the incomplete oxidation of carbon, is at present considered as perhaps the most dangerous of substances present in the sidestream smoke. According to Dusek and Girdano (1987), the sidestream smoke is richer in carbon monoxide than the midstream smoke, since the sidestream temperature is cooler and only incomplete oxidation of some constituents of smoke occurs at such low temperatures. They have further estimated that the smoking of a single cigarette releases about 25mg of carbon monoxide in the air surrounding the smoker. The level of carbon monoxide in smoke filled rooms often reaches 80 ppm and this is definetely hazardous for human health.

Carbon monoxide is harmful to the cardiovascular system and it affects smokers and nonsmokers alike. For those who have already developed a cardiovascular disease, the carbon monoxide of cigarette smoke is as dangerous as a poison. As already mentioned, the gas readily binds with haemoglobin of blood to form carboxyhaemoglobin and alters myocardial metabolism. It also interferes with oxygen delivery into cardiac tissues and produces myocardial infraction (Castelden, 1974). Carbon monoxide also stimulates the process of atherosclerosis, resulting in higher chances of development of thromboembolic disorders. Carbon monoxide reduces the cardiac work capacity of normal persons.

At present, low nicotine cigarettes are available in different countries but they are not of much value in prevention of smoke induced cardiac diseases because it is not possible to reduce the carbon monoxide content of these cigarettes though the nicotine content can be controlled.

(c) **Other gaseous compounds:** Among the other harmful gaseous compounds of cigarette smoke are formaldehyde, acetaldehyde, nitrogen oxides, sulphur oxides, volatile nitrosoamones, butane and ammonia. These gases may cause nausea and irritation of eye and noses to the non-smokers. These gases may also produce coughs and augment the breathing problems of persons suffering from asthma and other respiratory tract diseases, since these gases can immobilize the movement of the cillia of the respiratory tract (Surgeon General, 1988). Among the gases mentioned above, ammonia is most poisonous and is responsible for most of the respiratory problems that many smokers experience.

Hydrogen cyanide is another deadly poisonous chemical which every smokers inhales. In cigarette smoke its concentration is over a hundred and fifty times than what is considered safe in industry.

(d) **Arsenic:** A smoker who smokes about 20 cigarettes a day can dump into his system as much as 40 milligrams of arsenic each year. The arsenic is not present in the tobacco plant itself but comes from the lead arsenate, a very poisonous chemical which is used on the tobacco leaves as pesticide.

2.3 Nicotine

Nicotine-3- (1methyl-2 pyridine : 1- methyl-2- (3-pyridyl) pyrrolidine: - pyridyl - N - methyl pyrrolidine, $C_{10}H_{14}N_2$, Mol. wt. 162.23.

Tobacco contains about 2-8 % nicotine which is an oil,

volatile colourless alkaloid, combined with citric acid and malic acids.

It is present in cigarette smoke and is harmful to cardiovascular patients. Many smokers are not aware that nicotine is one ot the most powerful and lethal insecticides used by gardners.While the nicotine absorbed from a cigarette does not kill the smoker, there is little doubt that it slowly but surely brings about deterioration in his health and places him in greater risk of becoming a victim of several serious illness, including attacks (coronary thrombosis) (for details see section 2.4)

2.3.1 Pharmacological Actions

The complex and often unpredictable changes that occur in the body after administration of nicotine are due not only to its actions on a variety of neuroeffector and chemosensitive sites but also to the fact that the alkaloid can stimulate and desensitize receptors. The ultimate response of any one system represents the stimulation of stimulatory and inhibitory effects of nicotine. For example, the drug can increase the heart rate by excitation of sympathetic or paralysis of parasympathetic cardiac ganglin, and it can slow the heart rate by paralysis of sympathetic or stimulation of parasympathetic cardiac ganglin. In addition, the effects of the drug on the chemoreceptors of the carotid and aortic bodies and on medullary centres influence heart rate, as do also the cardiovascular compensatory reflexes resulting from changes in blood pressure caused by nicotine. Finally, nicotine elicits a discharge of epinephrine from the adrenal medulla, and this hormone raises blood pressure.

A. **Peripheral nervous system:** The major action of nicotine consists initially in transient stimulation and subsequently in a more persistent depression of all automatic ganglia. Small doses of nicotine stimulate the gangling cell directly and facilitate the transmission of impulses. When large doses of the drug are applied, the initial stimulation is followed very quickly by a blockade of transmission. Whereas stimulation of the ganglion cells coincides with their depolarization, depression of transmission by adequate doses of nicotine occurs both during the depolarization and after it has subsided. Nicotine also possesses a biphasic action on the adrenal medulla; small doses evoke the discharge of catecholamines, and large doses prevent their release in response to splanchnic nerve stimulation.

Nicotine causes the release of catecholamines in a number of isolated organs. This action results in a sympathomimetic response to nicotine that is blocked by drugs known to prevent the effects of catecholamines. The effects of nicotine on the neuromuscular juntion are similar to those ganglia. However with the exception of avian and denervated mammalian muscle, the stimulating phase is larger obscured by the rapidly developing paralysis. In the later stage, nicotine also produces neuromuscular blockade by receptor desensitization.

Nicotine, like acetyl cholines, is known to stimulate a number of action receptors. These include mechanoreceptors that respond to stretch or pressure of the skin mesentary, tongue, lung and stomach chemoreceptors and pain receptors. Prior administration of hexamethonium prevents the stimulation of the sensory receptors by nicotine, but has little, if any effect on the activation of the sensory receptors by physiological stimuli.

B. **Central nervous system:** Nicotine markedly stimulates the CNS. Appropriate doses produce tremors; with somewhat larger doses, the tremor is followed by convulsions. The excitation of respiration is a prominent action of nicotine; although large doses act directly on the medulla oblongata, smaller doses augment respiration reflexly by excitation of the chemoreceptors of the carotid and aortic bodies. Stimulation of the CNS is followed by depression, and death results from failure of respiration due to both central paralysis and peripheral blockade of muscles of respiration.

Nicotine induce vomitting by both central and peripheral actions. The central component of the vomitting responses is due to stimulation of the emetic chemoreceptor trigger zone in the area of postrema of the medulla oblogata. In addition, nicotine activates vagal and spinal afferent nerves that form the sensory input of the reflex pathways involved in the act of vomitting.

C. **Cardiovascular system:** When administered intravenously to the dog, nicotine characteristically produces an increase in heart rate and blood pressure. The later is usually a more sustained response. In general, the cardiovascular responses to nicotine are due to stimulation of sympathetic ganglia and the adrenal medulla together with the discharge of catecholamines from sympathetic nerve endings. Also contributing to the sympathomimetic response to nicotine is the activation of chemoreceptors of the aortic and carotid bodies, which reflexly results in vasoconstriction tachycardia and elevated blood pressure.

D. **Gastrointestinal tract:** The effects of the drug on the Gastrointestinal tract are due to parasympathetic stimulation. The combined activation of parasympathetic ganglia and cholinergic nerve endings result in increased tone and motor activity of the bowel. Nausea, vomiting and occasionally diarrhoea are observed following systemic absorption of nicotine in an individual who has not been exposed to nicotine previously.

E. **Exocrine glands:** Nicotine causes an initial stimulation of salivary and bronchial secretions that is followed by inhibition. Salivation caused by smoking is reflexly produced by the irritant smoke rather than by a systemic effect of nicotine.

2.3.2 Abrorption, Fate and Excretion

Nicotine is readily absorbed from the respiratory tract, buccal membrane, and skin. Several poisoning has resulted from percutaneous absorption. Being a relatively strong base, its absorption from the stomach is limited unless intragastric pH is raised. Intestinal absorption is far more efficient. Nicotine in chewing tobacco, because it is more slowly absorbed than inhaled nicotine, has a longer duration of effect. The average cigarette contains 8 to 9 mg of nicotine and delivers about 1 mg of nicotine systematically to the smoker; bioavailability can increase as much as threefold with intensity of puffing and technique of the smoker (Benowitz and Henningfield,1994). The nicotine patch is designed to produce relatively constant delivery of nicotine transdermally in order to reduce withdrawl symptoms during reaction of the lung. Its efficacy in producing abstinence from smoking is enhanced when linked to counselling and motivational thereby (Westman *et al.*, 1993).

Approximately 80 to 90 % of nicotine is allotted mainly in the liver but also in the kidney and lung. A significant fraction of inhaled nicotine is metabolized by the lung. Cotinine is the major metabolite with nicotine - 1 - N - Oxide and -hydroxy cotinine and conjugated metabolites found in lesser quantities (Benowiz and Jacob, 1994). The profile of metabolites and the rate of metabolism appear to be similar in the smoker and nonsmoker. The half-life of nicotine following inhalation or parenteral administration is about 2 hrs. Both nicotine and its metabolites are rapidly eliminated by the kidney. The rate of urinary excretion of nicotine is dependent upon the pH of the urine, excretion diminishes when the urine is alkaline. Nicotine is also excreted in the milk of lactating women who smoke, the milk of heavy smokers may contain 0.5 mg per litre.

2.3.3 **Toxicity**

(a) **Acute Nicotine Poisoning:** Poisoning from nicotine may occur from accidentally ingestion of insecticide sprays in which nicotine is present as the effective agent or in children from ingestion of tobacco products. The acutely fatal dose of nicotine for an adult is probably about

60 mg of the base. Smoking tobacco usually contains 1% to 2% nicotine. Apparently, the gastric absorption of nicotine from tobacco taken by mouth is delayed because of slowed gastric emptying so that vomiting caused by the central effect of the initially absorbed fraction may remove much of the tobacco remaining in the gastro-intestinal tract.

(b) **Therapy:** Vomitting should be induced with the syrup of ipecac or gastric lavage should be preformed. Alkaline solutions should be avoided. A slurry of activated charcoal is then passed through the tube and left in the stomach. Respiratory assistance and treatment of shock may be necessary.

2.3.4 **Addiction:**

Why is it that people who smoke cannot give it up easily? WHO statistics has shown that 50% of the adult male population is addicted to one or the other form of tobacco use (WHO, 1982,83). The question of whether nicotine is addictive has been open to considerable scientific and public discussion. Although it can serve as a positive reinforced in several animal species, including man, nicotine is thought to be a weak reinforce in comparison with addictive drugs such as cocaine and heroin and has been argued to be habit forming but not addictive.

However nicotine has been thought to be a highly addictive drug and a powerful stimulant. Like alcohol, nicotine first stimulats the smoker's system and creates an illusion of well being and releases from tension, but almost immediately depresses both mind and body. The natural reaction for the smoker to arch out for yet another cigarette in order to prolong the illusion of well being and the vicious circle of stimulation and depression continues and the physical condition of the body deteriorates in the long run.

The view that nicotine is a powerful addictive drug was summarised in the influential US Surgeon General's report in 1988. This assessment has been strengthened by further research showing similarities between nicotine and a number of drugs of addiction including cocaine, amphetamine and heroin (Stolerman, 1995). But it was not always thus, and there remains the view that nicotine- and thus smoking is not addictive, with all that implies for anti-smoking campaigns.

(a) **Mechanism of Action:**

However, recent research proof that nicotine is indeed addictive in rats receiving small intravenous doses of nicotine- corresponding the doses which the animals will self-administer- there is highly selective increase in the release of the neuro-transmitter dopamine, and an activation of energy metabolism in the precise region of the forebrain that is similarly activated by cocaine, amphatamine and morphine.

The part of the brain involved is the nucleus accumbens, a small dopamine-rich brain region situated ventrally at the head of the striatum, which plays a crucial role in the rewarding effects of these addictive drugs.

Animals can be trained to self administer such drugs directly into the nucleus accmubens or into the ventral regimental area in midbrain from which the dopaminergic fibres inncravating the molecules accumbens originate. Measurement of dopamine releases made by means of microdialysis probes in the intact brains of conscious animals show a selective releases of dopamine in the nucleus accumbens in response to administration of psychostimulants and morphine. Furthermore, damage to the dopamine fibres in the nucleus accumbens in animals trained to self-adminster addictive drugs leads to extinction of this behaviour.

It has been known for sometime that nicotine can mimic the addictive psychostimulants in causing dopamine release from the nucleus accumbenses (Clarke,1990, Imperato *et al.*, 1989). The new results and a further refinement, is that separate measurement of dopamine release and energy metabolism (measured by accumulation of radiolabelled deoxyglucose) were made in the subdivisions of the nucleus accumbens knows as the "shell" and the "core". The shell is a region whose connections are largely with the limbic system and which can be viewed as part of an "extended amygdala", while the core has connection largely with the motor systems of the basal ganglia (Heimer,1991). Put another way, the relationship mean that the shell may be a key link between midbrain and forebrain, playing a role in motivational and emotional functions, while the core is involved in the coordination of movements.

It was reported that cocaine, amphetamine and morphine provoked a selective release of dopamine from the shell region of nucleus accumbens in rat brain (Pontieri *et al*, 1995), and that this was accompained by a similarly selective increase in energy metabolism in this brain region (Pontieri *et al*, 1994). Nicotine mimics precisely these effects, with highly selective effects on the shell region of nucleus accumbens, thus placing it in the same category as the other psychostimulants and opiates in terms of its effects on a key structure in the brain circuits involved in drug reward and drug seeking behaviour (Pontiere *et al*., 1996).

Many questions remain unanswered, what, for instance, are the consequences of activation of dopamine receptors by the drug-induced release of dopamine in the nucleus accumbens shell? (Pontieri *et al*, 1994). Findings published earlier this year from a group at the University of Yale suggest that stimulation of both D^1 and D^2 dopamine-receptor subtypes may be important (Self *et al*,1996). Their finding in animals implied that drugs that act to stimulate D^1 receptors could partially substitute for cocaine, whereas drugs which stimulate D^2 receptors appeared to provoke further drug-seeking behaviour. These results suggest that D^1 dopamine agonists might have a therapeutic use in treating withdrawl from addictive drug, while D^2 antagonists might help to reduce craving.

The brain receptors targeted by nicotine are more clearly understood. More than 90% of high-affinity binding sites for nicotine in mammalian brain are accounted for by a subtype of the acetylcholine nicotonic receptor containing 4 and 2- subunits. This neuronal nicotinic receptor differs from that found in muscle in displaying a much higher affinity for nicotine and related alkaloids.

The precise anatomical location of the nicotinic receptors that are responsible for its effect on nucleus accumbens, however, is not known. Both the nucleus accumbens itself and the ventral tegmental area possess a high density of nicotinic receptors, and nicotine may act either to stimulate activity in the ventral tegmental dopamine neurons or locally on dopamine nerve terminals in the nucleus accumbens to provoke dopamine release. Whether the accompanying increases in energy metabolism is triggered directly by the released dopamine is also now known, although this would seem likely, as the same change is seen in response to other psychostimulants that act to increase dompamine release.

(b) **Addiction Still a Controversy**

In economically developed countries, about three million people die each year from smoking, half of them before the age of 70, and these represent about 20% of all deaths. Cancers of eight different sites are directly associated with smoking, and six other potentially fatal diseases are also judged to be caused by smoking. There is no doubt that smoking kills, and attitudes to the habit have changed radically in the past 30 years.

For centuries since its introduction, however, tobacco smoking was regarded as neither harmful nor addictive. Scientific evidences in the 1950's and 1906's persuaded most people that smoking was harmful- but it was still not considered to be addictive, despite the high relapse rate in smokers who attempt to stop (more than 95 % within 12 months, similar to rate for heroin addicts). By the 1980's however, the evidence that nicotine is addictive became more and more persuasive, leading to the Surgeon General's report in 1988 and the hard-hitting attack on nicotine addiction in young people by the Head of the Food and Drug administration in last four years.

The controversy of nicotine as addictive drug is still not clear. Recent findings by some of the experts have questioned the above experiments. It must be remembered that the smoker's habit is very complex and is associated with many factors. These include flavour, smoke, personality, mood and the social setting one happens to be in which may involve having in alcoholic drink, being under stress or, among other things, having fun. Perhaps most important however, is the rapid rise in blood levels of nicotine associated with inhalation of tobacco smoke (Pontieri,1996). Indeed, an important characteristic of all drugs that produce dependency is the time between behavioural administration (smoking a cigarette) and the drug's entry into the brain.

The US Food and Drug administration has recently approved the over-the-counter sale of transdermal nicotine as a smoking cessation aid, a drug delivery system designed to avoid the harmful chemicals found in cigarette smoke. The slower absorption of nicotine offered by the transdermal nicotine patch relative to tobacco products should substantially reduce the likelihood of nicotine dependence in users of the patch. For example, a recent doubleblind, placebo-controlled study investigating the therapeutic potential of the transdermal nicotine patch for ulcerative colitis found little evidence for nicotine withdrawl symptoms following discontinuation of the patch, despite 26 weeks of daily applications of 15 mg nicotine patches (Thomas *et al*,1995).

Cigarette smoking is clearly a major health problem, and decreasing its use is a worldwide effort, but there is also growing body of evidence to indicate that nicotine has therapeutic properties. [see section 2.4.3] Nicotine improves cognitive function and may reduce the symptoms of certain neuropsychiatric disorders such as Tourette's syndrome and attention deficit/hypereactivity disorder (Sanberg Levin,1996). But many of these efforts will be hampered if the role of nicotine in cigarette smoking is overemphasized without acknowledging the essential differences between nicotine, tobacco and other drugs of abuse.

2.3.5 **Withdrawl:**

As discussed earlier nicotine has both stimulant and depressant actions.The smoker feels alert yet there is some muscle relaxation. Smokers typically report that the first cigarette of the day after a night of abstinence gives the "best" feeling. Smokers who return to cigarette after a period of abstinence may experience nausea if they return immediately to their previous dose. Persons naive to the effects of nicotine will experience nausea at low nicotine blood level and smokers will experience nausea if nicotine levels are raised above their accustomed levels.

In dependent smokers, there is evidence that the urge to smoke correlated with a low blood nicotine level as though smoking were a means to achieve a certain nicotine level and thus avoid withdrawl symptoms. Some smokers even wake up during the night to have a cigarette, which ameliorates the effect of low nicotine blood levels that could disturb sleep. If the nicotine level is maintained artificially by a slow intravenous infusion, there is a decrease in the number of cigarette smoked and in the number of puffs (Goodman and Gilman, 1996). Thus smokers may be smoking to acheive the reward of nicotine effects, to avoid the pain of nicotine withdrawl or most likely, a combination of the two.

Nicotine withdrawl symptoms are listed below:

Nicotine Withdrawl Syndrome:

1. Irritability, impatience, hostility
2. Anxiety
3. Dysphorice or depressed mood
4. Difficulty concentrating
5. Restlessness
6. Decreased heart rate
7. Increased appetite or weight gain

Depressed mood (dysthymic disorder, affective disorder) is associated with nicotine dependence, but it is not known whether depression predisposes one to begin smoking or develops during the course of nicotine dependence. Depression significantly increases during smoking withdrawl and this is cited as one of the reason for relapse.

Nicotine can be taken as smoke, snuff, chewing or gum tobacco. As because nicotine gum and patch do not achieve peak levels in the blood as seen with smoking, they do not produce the same magnitude of effects as smoking. If gum tobacco is used to replace smoking in smokers, they would be able to transfer their dependence to the alternative delivery system and gradually reduce the daily nicotine dose with minimal symptoms. Hence, after few weeks of trail, the smokers may slowly withdraw himself from smoking.

2.4 Smoking and Health

2.4.1 Smoking and Cancer:

Smoking dried tobacco leaves is basically the best and easiest means of administering nicotine, just as smoking opium is a means obtaining morphine. As discussed earlier, nicotine, however, is but a small component of cigarette smoke, which contains more than 4,700 chemical compounds, including 43 cancer-causing substances. Condensates of tobacco smoke suspended in acetone and applied to the skin of mice for long periods cause papillomas or carcinomas at the site. Toxins in cigarette smoke cause breaks in the DNA of cultured human lung cells. In some cases, these carcinogens greatly accelerate the mutation rate in dividing cells, which in turn can lead to tumor formation.

Higher incidence of oral cancer in India is ascribed to smoking and chewing tobacco (Bhide and Pratap,1981;

Murdia and Mehta,1982). The carcinogenecity of smoked tobacco in form of cigarette, cigar, bidi, hukah is attributed to benzo(a)pyrene present in the smoke inhaled but that of its components before smoking is suspected to be due to several compounds. The central committee on Food Standards has found that *Pan Masala* (Mixture of betel mut, catechu, lime, cardamon, flavouring agents and tobacco) *zarda* (Flavoured tobacco balls or flakes) and *gutka* (Poorman's pan masala) cause hardening of the fibrous tissues of the mouth (Fibrosis) and cancer of the mouth.

Unfortunately for smokers, no threshold level of exposure to the toxins has been found. What is clear is that years of cigarette smoking vastly increases the risk of developing several fatal conditions. In addition to being responsible for more than 85% of lung cancer, smoking is associated with cancers of mouth, pharynx, larynx, stomach, pancreas, uterine, cervix, kidney, ureter, bladder, and colon. Cigarette smokings is thought to cause about 14% of all leukemias and 30% of new cases of cervical cancer in women. All told, cigarette smoking is responsible for 30% of all deaths from cancer and clearly represents the most important preventable cause of cancer in the US today.

Smoking also increases the risk of cardiovascular disease, including stroke, sudden death, heart attack, peripheral vascular disease and aortic aneurysm. Cigarette has been found to cause almost 1,80,00 deaths from cardiovascular disease in the U.S. in 1990. Components of cigarette smoke damage the inner lining of blood vessels, which can lead to the development of atherosclerosis. The toxins can also stimulate occlusive elements in coronary arteries, thus promoting clots to form and triggering spasms that close off the vessels. In this regard the smoking of a single cigarette can profoundly disturb blood flow to the heart in patients with existing coronary artery diesease.

Furthermore, cigarette smoking is the leading cause of pulmonary illness and death in the U.S. In 1990 smoking has been found to cause more than 84,000 deaths from pulmonary disease, mainly resulting from such problems as pneumonia, emphysema, bronchitis and influenza.

Passive smoking: The breathing of sidestream smoke (emitted from the burning tobacco between puffs) of smoke inhaled by the smoker- poses a similar health risk (for details refer to section 2.4.4)). A 1992 Environmental Protection Agency (EPA) report emphasized the dangers,especially of sidestream smoke. This type of smoke contains more particles of smaller diameter and is therefore more likely to be deposited deep in the lungs. On the basis of this report, the EPA has classified environmental tobacco smoke as a "group A" carcinogen, to which radon, asbestos, arsenic and benzene belong.

Of the estimated 53,000 deaths in the U.S. caused by passive smoking, 37,000 come from associated heart diseases.A non smoker living with a smoker has a 30% higher risk of death from ischemic heart disease or myocardial infarction. Lung cancer risk has also skyrocketed. Any exposure from a spouse who smokes is associated with at least a 30% excess of risk of lung cancer. Increasing daily amounts and the number of years of smoking significantly heighten the risk. The figure jumps to 50% if the spouse has been smoking four packs a day for 20 years. Another recent study points out that 17% of the cases of lung cancer among nonsmokers can be attributed to exposure to high levels of tobacco smoke during childhood and adolescence.

The health consequences of smoking among women are of special concern because of the deleterious effect on reproductive. Unfortunately, the fastest-growing segment of smokers in the U.S. is women younger than 23 years. Smoking reduces fertility, spurs the rate of spontaneous abortions and stillbirths, can cause excessive bleeding during pregnancy and results in lower birth weights in infants. Moreover, children of smokers do not grow as large or attain the same level of educational achievement as unexposed children.

Smoking is a significant cause of cardiovascular diseases and strokes in women, especially if they also use oral contraceptives. Lung cancer has now surpassed breast cancer as the primary cause of death from cancer among women. In 1993 lung cancer claimed an estimated 56,000 deaths, whereas breast cancer took 46,000 lives.

Tobacco smoking, chewing and eating is the largest single cause of preventable early death. (Table2).

Table - 2

Tobacco Kills

Tobacco smoking kills 30 lakh (3 Million) people per year over all over the world. In USA 5% of the total deaths are due to alcohol, 2% due to drugs, and 25% due to smoking. In India tobacco kills 10 lakh (1million) people per year through:

* Lung Cancer	* Mouth Cancer
* Chronic Bronchitis	* Voice Box Cancer
* Heart Diseases	* Food Pipe Cancer
* Paralysis	* Stomach Cancer
* High Blood Pressure	* Urine Bladder Cancer
* Gangrene of Limbs	* Cervix Cancer of Women

In addition, Betel-quid chewing, and consumption of Khaini, Mawa, Mishri, Godakhu and Paan Masala cause the largest number of Mouth Cancers. Millions of smokers suffer from Cripple Lungs and Overstrained Hearts.

Effects on Children:-

* More and frequent coughs, colds, pneumonia, asthma, head aches, tonsillitis, ear aches, stomach aches, bad breath, bad teeth.
* Higher rates of absence from school and reduction of fitness levels, reaction time, vigilance and concentration.
* Increased risk of death from lung cancer, heart diseases, bronchitis and mouth cancer later on in life.
* Delayed physical and mental growth.

Effects on Women:-

* Wrinkled skin, fragile hair, red eyes, bad smell, discoloured teeth and hoarse voice.
* Low fertility, higher still births, more abortions, early menopause, and low calcium in bones- fractures.

Effects on Passive smokers (enforced smoking):-

* Inhale other person's smoke either from burning end of cigarettes, bidis or from exhaled smoke of smokers, children get smoke from parents, and wife from husband or vice versa.
* Higher risk of cancer lung, heart diseases and chronic bronchitis.
* Risk in children leading to recurrent respiratory infection, asthma, reduced lung functioning, poor weight gain, general ill health and children are also more likely to develop the smoking habit.

High price of cigarette, bidi and tobacco is a drain on the family income

Effect on the Work Place:-

* Smokers take 50% more sick leaves, and 50% of smokers are more likely to be hospitalised.
* Smokers has twice as maybe on-the-job accidents.
* Smokers waste 2.6% of their working hours.
* Smoking necessities increased cleaning and repairs resulting in extra costs at the working place.
* Passive smoking can cause significant irritation, discomfort and health risk.

Nicotine the Culprit:-

* Tobacco contains hundreds of poisonous substances-nicotine, carbon monoxide, and tar-which are dangerous.

* Nicotine to start with, produces dizziness, vomitting, diarrhea etc. Tolerance to these develops later. Deprivation of tobacco causes irritation, craving, inability to concentrate and sleeplessness, children should be aware of these symptoms.

* Increases heart rate and blood pressure, causes loss of smelling and tasting faculties, and reduces both physical and mental performances.

* Carbon monoxide reduces oxygen of blood and tar causes cancer.

Remember the economic losses:-

* Loss of land needed for growing food for the ever increasing population.

* Loss of forests and consequent spread of deserts because of the large amount of wood needed for curing tobacco (burning).

* Cost of caring for those suffering from the effects of tobacco smoking, chewing and eating. Money spent on their treatment.

* India earns Rs. 15,515 Million (Rs.1,515 corers) by way of excise duty and spends about Rs. 22,365 million on treating the disease caused by tobacco, besides loss in productivity due to ill health, premature deaths, low efficiency and disability, which comes to

about Rs. 30,000 million (Rs.3,000 crores) per year.

(Source: Indian Society on Tobacco and Health, New Delhi)

2.4.2 Side Effects of Smoking:

(a) Facial Wrinkles: Recent researches have indicated that cigarette smoke can cause a variety of diseases that have been related previously with other agents. Smoking can cause increased risk of developing facial wrinkles.

Researchers from the Kaiser Permanent Medical Centre in Oakland, California have linked smoking with facial wrinkles among whites and say that women may be more susceptible than men (American Journal of Public Health, vol. 85, No.1). The research team led by Virginia L Ernster, decided on whites-only as the African-American and Asian skins are relatively less prone to wrinkling. The results from their study based on 1136 subjects indicate that smokers have a two to three fold risk of developing facial wrinkling compared to non-smokers. The exception to this rule being men aged 60-69 years. Earlier studies have also established the link between smoking and facial wrinkling but they handled relatively small population samples.

The Oakland study-revealed that the wrinkling risk was greater for women smokers compared to men. The risk of developing wrinkles appeared to increase after 10 pack-years (a pack-year is the number of cigarette packs consumed daily multiplied by years smoked) of smoking in women as compared to 20 pack-years in men. Also, the former male smokers faced no increased risk whereas it was twofold for women.

The researchers say that wrinkling in smokers could be due to drying or irritating effect of the smoke on the skin. Or, it could be a result of vascular or connective tissue damage in the skin caused by the absorption of cigarette smoke. Earlier studies have shown that smoking acutely decreases the blood flow in the skin.

The Oakland study being the largest of its kind, researchers hope that their results would encourage young people to quit smoking. They say that they would like the wrinkling effect of smoking printed on cigarette packs as a warning to smokers.

(b) Chromosomal Irregularities: Smokers the elderly or babies whose mothers smoked during pregnancy are most likely to have irregularities in their chromosomes and greater risk of developing certain types of cancer. James Tucker and his colleagues at the Lawrence Liverrmore National Laboratory in California have used a technique called chromosome painting to detect damaged stretches of human DNA. His team are trying to explain why smokers and elderly people have a greater risk of developing certain types of cancer.

Tucker's team identified disrupted DNA sequences using strands of DNA which cling to specific chromosomes because their sequence matches a characteristic stretch of human genetic material. The researchers used these probes to colour-code the chromosomes in human white blood cells. They attached pink fluorescent dyes to some of these DNA probes, which stained some chromosomes pink. They then added a dye that made the remainder fluoresce blue. Whenever the researchers saw a "hybrid" chromosome that was part pink and part blue, they knew that a piece of one chromosome had broken off and joined another by mistake- a phenomenon called translocation.

Tucker's group took blood samples from people aged 20 to 80, as well as from the umbilical cords of new born babies. The researchers found that translocation were low rated in young people, appearing on average in one out of every 400 white blood cells. But in people over 50, these mistakes were ten times as common. Smokers also had more translocations than non smokers and if a mother smoked during pregnancy, the number of translocations in her new born baby's blood was 50 % higher than in the babies of non smokers.

Translocations in chromosomes have been implicated in cancer. Virtually every kind of cancer cell has these chromosomes rearrangement, says Tucker. This can happen if breakages damage genes that control cell division, causing uncontrolled proliferation of cells. One particular translocation, for example is thought to be involved in the development of chronic myeloid leukaemia.

The increased DNA damage in smokers and their babies, says Tucker, is probably caused by one or more of the many hundreds of substances found in cigarette smoke. Older people may be less able to repair damaged DNA, and therefore are more susceptible to DNA damage from mutagens in the environment such as chemicals or ionising radiation from the Sun.

Tucker says that chromosome painting could be used to monitor the DNA of people who have been exposed to radiation or harmful chemicals. If scientists can estimate the extent of the DNA damage in these people it may be possible to predict their risk of developing cancer. With that in mind Tucker's group is studying blood cells from people exposed to radiation during the Chernobyl disaster, and agricultural workers in Minnesota who have worked with pesticides.

2.4.3 Benefits of Smoking

Even though smoking causes a number of diseases in the human body, it may have some beneficial effects also. Like alcohol, nicotine temporarily reduces tension in some muscles of the body, stimulates some sensitive nerves, increases the rate at which the heart beats and heart's output of blood and causes increase in the flow of hormones from the gland. Recent findings indicate that because of these, cigarette smoke can protect against a number of diseases and even cause enhancement of memory but the researchers are yet to exactly clarify and establish the above facts.

(a) Smoking and Brain Disorders: A number of epidemiological studies have reported that smokers suffer fewer cases than non-smokers of the progressive brain disorder, Parkinson's diseases. The same has been found for Azheimer's diseases, the common form of dementia, and the inflammatory gut diseases ulcerative colitis. Smoking also appears to protect against rheumatoid arthritis, some cancers and other conditions (New Scientist, 9 Oct., 1993, P.14).

Many scientist believe these studies open important avenues for research that could reveal the mechanisms of these diseases and new treatments. But strong evidence also exists that, because of the stigma attached to smoking, researchers, funding bodies and drug companies have failed to follow up these leads.

Epidemiologists began to find apparently beneficial effects of smoking in the late 1960s when a study showed that American military veterans with Parkinson's diseases were less likely to be smokers. Although other studies produced contrary or equivocal findings, the weight of evidence suggests that smokers are 50% less likely to develop Parkinson's diseases than those who have never smoked.

In the mid-1980s a similar effect was spotted for Alzheimer's diseases, although, again, later studies have produced varying results. Some found that smokers are 70% less likely to develop the diseases than abstainers; in others, smokers had no advantage. The most consistent finding of a reduced risk in smokers has been found in inherited Alzheimer's diseases.

Findings such as these usually send epidemiologists, molecular biologists and neurologists scuttling for theories to explain them and sure enough, ideas have emerged to show how smoking can endow protection. One theory suggests that Parkinson's diseases is triggered by environmental toxins. Caroline Tanner, of the California Parkinson's foundation in San Jos, speculates that something in cigarette smoke protects against these toxins.

In Alzheimer's interest has focused on the ability of nicotine to improve attention and the brain's ability to process information, although this is unlikely to explain a protective effect.

The epidemiological evidence suggests that there is something in the cigarette smoking smoke, in the nicotine, that directly relates to the manner in which brain cells die. It's not just supporting the cells that are still there but preventing the cells from dying in the first place.

One theory that could explain this preventive effect stems from a tie-up between nicotine and acetylcholine, one of the vital chemical that relay impulses from one brain cell to the next. Acetylcholine stimulates two different types of "receptors" on these cells, one that can be artificially stimulated by a substance called maucarine, the other nicotine.

Nicotine has the added effect of increasing the number of the nicotine receptors on brain cell. When researchers found that alzheimer's patients had depleted number of acetylcholine receptors in their brain, they questioned whether nicotine's actions might stop brain function deteriorating.

But why should medical researchers be so reluctant to study the apparent effects of smoking? One reason given is that the epidemiological results are not all they appear to be.

People who develop Parkinson's may have a genetic predisposition to the diseases that also makes them less likely smoke. Yet another theory is that a larger than normal proportion of smokers die young from diseases induced by cigarettes, so it may not be surprising that a smaller than normal proportion of elderly smokers develop Parkinson's and Alzheimer's.

There is no doubt that in some cases the epidemiological evidence conflicts, and it may be that research showing as beneficial is just wrong. The work emphasises the need for more research. Even though medical research are making effort to disprove the benefits of smoking, attempts must be made by tobacco industries to give more stress on the above research.

Over the years, the tobacco industry has spent large sums of money on research into smoking and nicotine. A look at the scientific literature shows cigarette company funding often acknowledged after epidemiological studies and research on possible mechanisms. But however tobacco companies' research efforts have never been wholehearted because they fear it would confirm the "dependence-producing potential" of nicotine. If nicotine's value has been besmirched by tobacco, it is now having something of a renaissance. The impetus has come out, however, through attempts to explain the epidemiological effects of smoking, but from basic neurological findings. What has turned everybody back on again is the nicotinic receptor playing a role in neuroprotection. If you adminster nicotine to a damaged animal brain, it recovers much faster. This back-ups the notion that nicotine prevents the degeneration in alzheimer's diseases.

This work and the epidemiological research may reveal

once and for all whether nicotine- and hence smoking has a beneficial effect. But the question remains: should this research have been carried out sooner and what about all the other diseases smoking apparently protects against! These points should be dealt with separately by the Government and industry.

(b) Smoking and memory: The first discussion linking the enhancement of memory with the use of tobacco almost certainly occured long before tobacco was introduced to western society. In 1659, Dr. Giles Eveard wrote: "...to strengthen the memory the smoke is excellent taken by the nostrils, for it is properly belonging to brain, and it is easily conveyed into the cells of it and it cleaneth that from all filth (for the brain is the metropolis of the fregme, as Hypocrites teacheth us.....) from Pancreas; or the universal medicine, being a Discovery of the wonderful virtues of Tobacco taken in a pipe, with its operation and use both Physick and Chyrugery."

Although nearly all of the "wonderful venues of smoke" have now been disproved, the theory that nicotine enhances some forms of memory has remained undebated (Levin,1992). The underline mechanisms are still unknown, but Gray *et al*, 1996, provide evidence that nicotine increases the strength of synoptic communication between neurons in the hippocampus- a centre for learning and memory.

Many groups have examined the cellular events that control the strength of connection (Synapses) between nerve cells in the hippocampus (Squire and Lindlaub, 1990), and these studies have provided insight into the basic processes that are thought to underlie learning and memory. Hippocampal neurons express several classes of nicotonic acetylcholine receptors (nAChRs), and there is a differential subcellular distribution of the distinct nAChR subclasses (Alknodon, *et al*, 1997). Furthermore nicotinic cholinergic systems are believed to be important in memory- nicotine has a memory- enhancing effect, and there is a loss of cholinergic innervation from the basal fore-brain in pathologies that affect memory, such as Alzheimer's diseases.

Gray *et al*, 1996 shows that at the concentrations of the nicotine detected in arterial blood during smoking, there is enhanced gutamate-mediated transmission of nerve impulses in hippocampal cultures. They also show that nicotine increases the level of intracellular calcium measured directly from presynaptic terminals in hippocampal slices, providing the best evidence to date. The nAChRs that mediate enhanced neurotransmitter releases are localized to these presynaptic terminals. Such high-resolution analysis constitutes a significant advance in our understanding of the potent effects of nicotine at an important site in the brain.

2.4.4 Passive Smoking:

Smoking a cigarette produces two main kinds of smoke (i) what the smoker draws into his mouth (usually into his lungs) called mainstream smoke and (ii) smoke which issues into the atmosphere when cigarette is held smouldering is called passive smoking or side arm smoke. Side arm smoke is more dangerous because the volume of this smoke produced is double that of mainstream smoke, secondly, several chemicals in tobacco smoke are present in higher concentration in one side arm smoke, thirdly side stream smoke is unfiltered.

Passive smoking or the side arm smoking is often heavy and if continued over a lifetime, could give rise to the same alarming spectrum of diseases suffered by the smoker himself. About 50% of non smokers say that they suffer definite ill effects from passive smoking. Nonsmokers with allergic diseases like asthma suffer more when they are exposed to cigarette smoke. Similar is the case with non smoking patients with chronic angina pectoris, bronchitis and emphysema. Nitrosamines which are extremely powerful organ specific carcinogens, have been found to be present in side stream smoke.

In 1979 White and Froeb of the California University, San Diego, USA found that nonsmokers who had worked alongside smokers continually for some year together had poorer lung functions than nonsmokers without such exposure. A similar situation also observed with wives of smoking husbands and also children of smoking parents. Such passive smoking is unavoidable in cities. A significant nicotine content was found from the blood of nonsmokers from these crowded cities.

One should also note that passive smoking begins in the womb (by the unborn child) of the smoking pregnant woman and it can sufficiently damage the fetus. Researchers from Bristol Royal Hospital for sick children have reported that babies born to smoking mothers are smaller and going childhood with reduced weights and with some retarded academic pick-up. Further in women who smoke there is an increase in still births and neonatal death rates probably because of placental disorders. A report from the Edinborrough State College, Pennsylvania, says that nonsmoking women whose husbands are long cigarette smokers die on an average four year earlier than women married to nonsmokers.

Effect on cognitive functioning:

Passive smokers are prone to health risks like lung cancer, respiratory illness, abnormal functioning, small-always dysfunction etc. (Cotran *et al.*, 1989). For no fault of theirs, the nonsmokers have to inhale the cigarette smoke if they are in the ambience of cigarette smokers. Evidences show that it will risk their health. Despite health risk, does nonsmokers have any advantage psychologically, such as, aiding in concentration (Frankenhaeuser *et al.*, 1971), as in the case of smokers? Will it have any effect on their cognitive functioning? Only a few systematic investigations are available to know about the psychological functioning of passive smokers with focus on the cognitive processes. Oborne (1983) conducted an experiment to find out the cognitive effects of passive smoking. He tested 32 subjects in two situations, namely smoky and non smoky. He found that their performance deteriorated in smoky situation when compared with the performance in non smoky situation. In fact passive smoking adversely effects the cognitive processing on tasks, memory span for digits, digit symbol substitution, and accuracy of testimony.

To test this hypothesis, a similar experiment was carried out by several research scholars from the Department of Education, Osmania University, Hyderabad (Srinivas Kumar, 1994). When nonsmoking subjects of this experiment were exposed to one another, cigarette smoke, their performance on digit-symbol substitution test and on accuracy of testimony was deteriorated. The performance on the test of memory span for digits was comparatively similar for the subjects of both groups.

The performance deterioration on the above said tasks could be examined from two angles, namely, physiological, and psychological. From the physiological point of view, the influence of Carbon Monoxide, one of the constituent of cigarette smoke, could be considered in two ways. First carbon monoxide would impair oxygen supply to the tissues (Holbrook, 1987), as a result of which the performance might have been deteriorated. But Oborne (1983) suggested that this could not be a probable reason for the decrement in performance. Second, the carbon monoxide could also cause subtle impairment of central nervous system (Holbrook, 1987). Probably this could be one of the reasons for the performance deterioration because of the following reasons : the tasks administered to the subjects involved performance of different functions like immediate recall, auditory imagery and visual imagery at times (memory span for digits); immediate role recall, visual motor integration (digits-symbol substitution); vigilance, visual imagery (accuracy of testimony) (Freeman, 1976). These functions are performed in various regions of brain (especially in that cerebrtal cortex), one of the basic elements in central nervous system. When there is a subtle impairment in the central nervous system, automatically the functional efficiency of brain and constituents would be affected.

From the psychological point of view, the deterioration of performance of the subjects of experimental group of the tests may be attributed to the surrounding conditions. The confederate of smokers was present in the experimental room along with the experimenter. The smoke was also defused in the entire room. Therefore, it would be appropriate to discuss about the effect of smokers, and effect of cigarette smoke on the performance of subjects on the tests.

(i) Effects of smokers: because they were doing dummy scoring, it could be assumed that there was no direct effect of them on the subjects.

(ii) Effects of cigarette smoke: It was observed that some of the subjects closed their noses with handkerchiefs within a few minutes after entering the experimental room. Probably, the cigarette smoke caused annoyance and vexation too the subject. Apparently, some of the subjects have exhibited their annoyance by closing their noses by the use of handkerchiefs. Other might have simply tolerated the smoke despite annoyance. These feelings of annoyance and vexation could have resulted in the reduction of attention among the subjects thereby they were unable to answer the tests properly.

It is interesting to note that the performance of the subject of both groups is similar on the test of memory, span for digits. This similarity could be ascribed to the low level influence of the annoying agent, that is, the cigarette smoke, at an initial stage of testing, on the subjects of the experimental group. It is, therefore, concluded that the cognitive processing of passive smokers would be adversely affected by the smoke from cigarettes. However, experiments are required to know further about the effect of cigarette smoke on the central nervous system of passive smokers with focus on carbon monoxide.

2.5 Smoking Linked Morality

The most widely accepted estimates of tobacco-related deaths are based on a study done for the world Health Organisation by a special group of consultants led by Richard Peto of Oxford University. This estimates indicates that during this decade on an average three million people are likely to die in one year due to tobacco-related diseases. Two million of these deaths per year are likely to take place in developed countries and one million in less developed countries.

Keeping in view the one million deaths for all the developing countries, the widespread use of tobacco, poor treatment facilities and the size of India's population, it is likely that nearly one-third to one-fourth of the tobacco-related deaths in developing countries take place in India. Hence the likely number of tobacco-linked deaths in a year is likely to be around three lakh or so.

However, a recent study conducted by the Indian Council of Medical Research (ICMR), showed that about eight lakh Indian die every year due to cancer induced by tobacco use. If this is true, then this means that India probably has the highest number of tobacco-related deaths in the world.

Generally, the US has been regarded as one of the worst sufferers of heavy tobacco use. According to estimates for 1991, 400,000 Americans were likely to die prematurely from tobacco-induced diseases, including about 136,000 from lung cancer, 115,000 from coronary heart diseases and 60,000 from chronic obstructive lung disease. Thus, while cancer, specially lung cancer, is the most important disease linked to tobacco, there are many other tobacco- related diseases, which cause a large number of deaths.

Seen in this perspective, it is clear that the figure of eight lakh cancer-related deaths in India alone is a very alarming one, and if there are strong reasons to accept this figure, then the worldwide data for tobacco-related deaths will have to be revised and the case for restricting the use of tobacco, already very strong, will become stronger.

On the other hand, if it is found that the ICMR has overestimated the number of tobacco-related deaths in India, this cannot be used as an excuse to slacken the campaign against tobacco. Even a figure of about 3 lakh tobacco-related deaths in a year (which is in conformity with the existing world data) is alarming enough to justify the further strengthening of the campaigns against tobacco.

So far as the alarming nature of the health threat posed by tobacco is concerned, there is no real conflict between the worldwide data and the Indian data. Still the few existing anamolies need to be removed so that a stronger and more consistent base can be prepared for educational campaigns against tobacco.

According to the World Health Organisation 6 million new cases are reported to doctors every year and two-thirds of all cancer deaths are from developing countries.

The Central Health Education Bureau, however, believes that tobacco kills 30 lakh people annually the world over while in India alone it kills 10 lakh every year through the cancers of the voice box (larynx), food pipe (oesophagus), urinary bladder, cervix of the uterus, and due to high blood pressure and gangrene.

In 1992 out of a population of 862 million, India had 6,44,600 new cases of cancer of which 2,1,100 were related to tobacco which is about 4 % in case of men. Oral cancer alone hits 63,000 Indians annually, followed by cancer of the pharynx and the larynx which claim another 60,000 per annum, 20,000 more Indians die of heart attack annually because of the worsening of the patient's conditioning due to smoking.

According to the WHO, nearly 6 trillion cigarettes are consumed globally every year. 41% men and 21% women are smokers in the developing countries. While in the developed countries like the US, the incidence of smoking fell from 42$ in 1965 to 26% in 1991, the situation has been deteriorating in developing world. In 1990 out of 800 million Indians, 337 million above age of 10 years smoked. Obviously therefore 90% of the deaths from lung cancer are due to smoking. With 142 million men and 722 million women addicted to tobacco. India wins a silver medal for smoking while China grabs the gold, as 300 million smokers in China consume a mind bogging 1.6 trillion cigarettes every year. Even at the rate of increase in smokers, the number of deaths will touch a crore every year globally. In another thirty years a death in every three seconds.

Although there are 40 harmful ingredients among 4,000 chemicals in cigarette smoke, just one drop of nicotine, if injected is reported to kill a person. Consequently, smoking can enhance the chances of 23 other fatal diseases, apart from cancer.

Betel quid (Pan) chewing and consumption of Khaini, mawa, gudaku, pan masala, gutka etc. further lead to widespread oral cancer. Frequent chewing of pan accompanied by tobacco, catechu and calcium has made the coastal regions of Orissa, the world's largest pocket with maximum number of oral cavity cancer patients.

Pan is the sole factor responsible for widespread quid bed cancer in the tribal areas of Sundergarh, Bolangir, Kalahandi, and Western Orissa. In the triangular zone comprising Nayaguid, Puri and Pardeep every patient had been chewing at least 20 pans on an average a day for the last 15 years of so when diagnosed. Consequently Orissa accounts for 50% of all the oral cancers in the country. While chemical fertilisers used for ripening pan prematurely could be the culprit, in pan masala, the use of chemically treated tobacco, the major component, aggravates the diseases.

Reverting to smoking, a report warns that smokers have 50% chances of becoming impotent than non-smokers. In Delhi, the All India Institute of Medical Science and the Institute of Rotary Cancer Hospital are treating approximately 50,000 cancer patients every year. In India at the rate of 2.1 % about 5,500 fresh smokers are enrolled every day amongst street urchins and school and college students.

The elderly also face special harm from smoking. Among those older than 65, the rates of total mortality among current smokers are twice those among people who have never smoked. A 1992 Time magazine article noted that three life insurers owned by tobacco companies charge smokers nearly double for term insurance.

Smoking is associated with a variety of other ailments: cataracts, delayed healing of broken bones, periodontal maladies, predisposition of ulcer diseases, hypertension, brain haemorrhages and skin wrinkles to name just a few. (see section)

Recently some studies have suggested that cigarette smoking ameliorates symptoms of Alzheimer's diseases (refer to section 2.4.3 for details). It is not surprising that with its powerful effect on the central nervous system, nicotine may influence the condition. Yet methodological flaws palgue many of these studies. Moreover, other researchers suggest that smoking may increase the risk of Alzheimer's in that it accelerated the natural consequences of aging. With its many and potent toxins, cigarettes would in any case be an inappropriate vehicle for delivering nicotine should the compound ever prove valuable in treating Alzheimer's.

There is much go be gained by those who kick the habit. After a year, mortality from heart diseases drops halfway back to that of a nonsmokers; by five years, it drops to the rate of nonsmokers. A person's risk of lung cancer is cut in half in five years; by 10 years, it drops almost the rate of non-smokers. Such gains makes sense, however, only if smokers quit in time, before they show any signs of tobaccos's lethal effects.

Table: Deaths from preventable causes in the US in 1990

Cause	Estimated No. of deaths	% of total deaths
Tobacco	400,000	19
Diet/activity pattern	300,000	14
Alcohol	100,000	5
Microbial agents	90,000	4
Toxic agents	60,000	3
Firearms	35,000	2
Sexual behaviour	30,000	1
Motor vehicles	25,000	1
Illicit use of drugs	20,000	<1
Total	1,060,000	50

A recent British study suggests that one half of all regular smokers will die from their habit. Statistically, each cigarette robs a regular smoker of 5.5 minute of life. Fig-I shows how prolonged smoking catches up on life.

Fig. - I

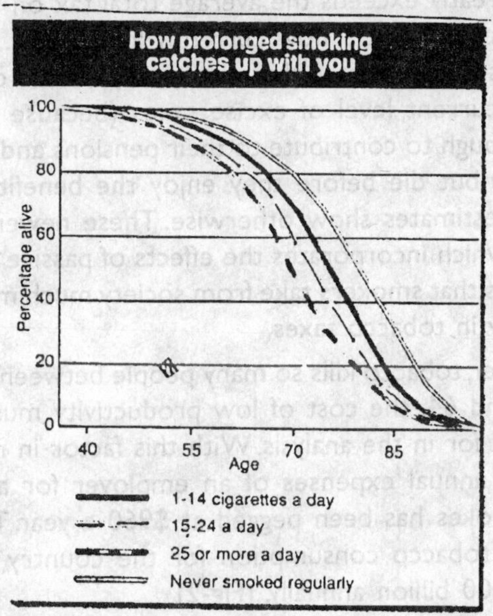

Tobacco also drains society economically. The University of California and the Centres for Diseases Control and Prevention (CDC) have calculated that the total health care cost to society of smoking-related diseases in 1993 was at least $ 50 billion, or $ 2.06 per pack of cigarettes-about the actual price of a pack in the US. That price figure greatly exceeds the average total tax on a pack of cigarettes in the US, now currently about 56%. Although a 1989 study suggested that smokers "pay their own way" at the current level of excise taxes (because they live long enough to contribute to their pensions and to social security but die before they enjoy the benefits), more recent estimates show otherwise. These newer calculations,, which incorporates the effects of passive smoking, indicates that smokers take from society much more than they pay in tobacco taxes.

Moreover, tobacco kills so many people between the ages of 35 and 64, the cost of low productivity must be accounted for in the analysis. With this factor in mind, the average annual expenses of an employer for a worker who smokes has been pegged at $960 a year. The total toll for tobacco consumption for the country may exceed $100 billion annually. (Fig-2)

Fig - 2

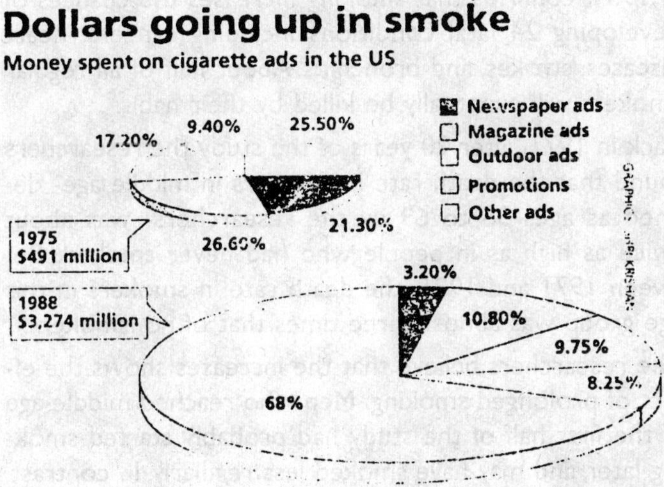

Source: Scientific American, May, 1995

Everyone knew it was bad, but no one realised just how bad. The world's longest running survey of smoking has found that the risks of the habit have been seriously underestimated. Researchers used to think that the death rate in middle age was about twice as high in cigarette smokers as in lifelong nonsmokers. Now they know it is almost three times as high. But there is some good news too: men who give up smoking at almost any age fare better than those who carry on, and those who give up under the age of 35 no worse overall than people who have never smoked.

The 40-year study of male British doctors, which began in 1951, confirms that smoking increases the chances of developing 24 fatal conditions including cancers, heart diseases, strokes, and bronchitis. About half of all regular smokers will eventually be killed by their habit.

Back in 1971, after 20 years of the study the researchers found that the death rate in smokers in middle age- defined as ages 35 to 69 by the researchers- was about twice as high as in people who had never smoked. Between 1971 and 1991, the death rate in smokers in this age group was almost three times that of nonsmokers.

The researchers believe that the increases shows the effect of prolonged smoking. Men who reached middle age in the first half of the study had probably started smoking later, and may have smoked less regularly. In contrast, regular smokers who reached middle age in the second half of the study had mostly taken up the habit in their later teens.

The study showed in 1950 that people with lung cancer were more likely to be smokers. The researchers asked all the registered doctors in Britain about their smoking habits. Of the 40,000 replied more than 34,000 were men so the study was restricted to them. The men's age ranged from their twenties to near retirement age. An analysis of the data in 1971 showed that about 10% had died; by 1991 roughly another 25% had died.

The team analysed the cause of death according to whether the doctors smoked or not, whether they smoked cigarettes, pipe or cigars, how many cigarettes they smoked daily, and whether and when they had given up. Tobacco was linked to increased deaths from cancers of the lung, mouth, throat, gullet, stomach, pancreas, bladder and rectum and a type of leukaemia called myeloid leukaemia. The links with rectal cancer and with myeloid leukemia were new and should be studied further. The death rate from asthma was more than twice as high among people who had smoked at some time than in those who had never smoked. Smoking also increased deaths from other diseases of which the person is suffering from.

2.5.1 Smoking Among Indians:

Contrary to widespread belief, there had been a sharp decline in cigarette smoking in India in the last one a half decades, according to data provided by International Tobacco Growers Association. The share of cigarette consumption out of the total tobacco consumed in 1992 declined to 20% from 21% in 1980s which itself was 2% lower than in the 1970s. Cigarette consumption has fallen to 16% in 1997, an all time low.

Indians smoked 86 million kgs. of cigarettes in 1981-82 but this came down to 66 million kg. in 1977, according to estimates by the National Council for Applied Economic Research (NCAER), New Delhi. Total tobacco consumption which includes bidis and other non smoking forms of tobacco increased from 309 million kg in the 1970s to 406 million kgs in the early 1980s. It stood at 417 million kg in 1997. The share of bidis in the total tobacco consumption went up from 29% in the 1970s to 47 % in the early 1980s to 50% in 1992. Estimates for 1994 revealed that bidis contributed a lion's share of 55 % of the total tobacco consumption in India.

However, figure for non smoking forms of tobacco have more or less been the same since the early 1980s. Its share in the total tobacco consumption came down by just 2% from the 1980s figure to the early 1990s. Its share has since been stagnant with this category contributing 120 million kg to Indian consumers last year.

To stop public smoking, the state health minister has introduced a bill christened as the "Delhi Prohibition of Smoking and Nonsmokers Health Protection Bill" in the legislative assembly. The first of its kind to be ever tabled by any state government in India. The objective of the bill is to discourage rising tobacco use in the capital and protect non-smokers from the effects of passive smoking. The bill disallows smoking in public places. The other salient features include banning of the sale of cigarettes, bidis and cigars to those below the age of 18 years and also within a radius of 100 m around educational institutions. The bill envisages a penalty of Rs. 100 for the first offence followed by Rs. 500 for subsequent offences. It also seeks to ban advertisements propagating smoking and sponsorship of tobacco products during a cultural or a sport event. The violators of this provision would have to pay a fine of Rs.500-1000 besides serving a 3 month prison sentence.

2.5.2 Smoking in Eastern Europe:

A 15 year old boy in Eastern Europe is twice as likely to

die before reaching 60 than his counterpart in the west. The difference in their prospects is largely the result of smoking, according to figures presented at the World conference on Tobacco and Health in Paris in 1994.

The statistics show that a man living in Europe's ex-communist countries today has a greater risk of dying before the age of 60 than men in most developing countries, including India, China and the Latin American Nations. According to the WHO, smoking is responsible for "About half" the deaths of men in middle age in Eastern Europe.

In this region an estimated 55 to 70 % of men and 30 to 35 % of women smoke. Since the fall of communism cigarette consumption has been rising, except during brief periods when some countries ran short of tobacco to make cigarettes. Predictions to the year 2000 suggest that consumption will continue to rise. In Poland, where cigarette sales per head are already among the highest, consumption between 1992 and 2000 is likely to increase by 3%. In Romania the expected increase is 46 %, although this will still leave the country lagging behind Poland.

Eastern Europe has some of the fastest growing rated of tobacco related illness. Every year around half a million people die from diseases caused by smoking. In Poland, the number of deaths from lung cancer is growing rapidly. In 1963, 16.5% of the deaths have reached 40.5%. According to Imperial Cancer Research Fund in Oxford by next year 41 % of deaths among Eastern Europeans men aged between 35 to 69 will be attributable to smoking. This :s twice the proportion in 1950.

Russia is currently in the midst of what researchers described as a "demographic catastrophe" more people are being dying than are being born. A growing number of deaths are related to smoking, and experts in Paris claimed that the chances of improvement are slim. In 1988 multinational tobacco firms controlled 3% of the market there. Now they control more than half the factories making cigarette. The Western cigarette companies that now dominate the market are targeting women and adolescents.

Former communist bloc is the world's second largest market for cigarettes after Asia. In 1988, multinational tobacco firms controlled 3% of the market there. Now they control more than half the factories making cigarettes. The number of deaths per year from smoking in the former socialist countries from 1955 to 1995 has doulered.

2.5.3 Smoking in Adolescents:

National surveys collected the ages at which people started smoking. The 1955 current population survey (CPS) was the first to query respondents for this information, although only summary date survive. Beginning in 1970, however the national health Interview Surveys (NHIS) included this question in some polls. Answers from all the surveys were combined to produce a sample of more than 165,000 individuals. Using a respondent's age at the time of the survey and the reported age of initiation, the year the person began smoking could be determined. Dividing the number of adolescents (defined as those 12 to 17 years old) who started smoking during a particular interval by the number who were legible to begin at the start of the interval set the initiation rate for that group.

Mass marketing campaigns began as early as the 1880s which boosted tobacco consumption sixfold in 1990. Much of the rise was attributed to a greater number of people smoking cigarettes, as opposed to using cigars, pipes, snuff or chewing tobacco. Marketing strategies included painted bill-boards and an extensive distribution of coupons, which a recipient could redeem for the cigarettes and a variety of other premiums. Some brands included soft-porn pictures of women in the packages. Such tactics inspired outcry from educational leaders concerned about their corrupting influence on teenage boys. 13% of the male surveyed in 1955 who reached adolescence between 1890 and 1910 commenced smoking by 18 years of age, compared with almost no females.

The power of targeting advertising is more apparent if one considers the men born between 1890 and 1899. In 1912, when many of these men were teenagers, the R.J. Reynolds Company launched the Camel brand of cigarettes with a revolutionary approach. In the months before the Camel debut, every city and helmet in the country was bombarded with print advertising. According to the 1955 CPS, initiation by age I for males in this group jumped to 21.6 %, a two thirds increase over those born before 1890. The NHIS initiation rate also reflected this change. For adolescent males, it went up from 2.0 % between 1910 and 1912 to 4.9 % between 1918 and 1921.

It was not until the mid-1920s that social moves permitted cigarettes advertising to focus on women (public clamour forced a 1919 ad aimed at women by Lorillard Company to be withdrawn). In 1926 a poster depicted women imploring smokers of Chesterfield Cigarettes to "Blow Some My Way". The most successful crusade, however, was for Luck Strikes, which urged women to "Reach for a Lucky instead of a Sweet". The 1955 CPS data showed that 7% of the women who were adolescents during the mid-1920s had started smoking by age 18, compared with only 2% in the preceding generation of female adolescents. Initiation rates from the NHIS data for adolescent girls were observed to increase threefold, from 0.6 % between 1922 and 1925 to 1.8% between 1930 and 1933. In contrast, rates for males rose only slightly.

The next major boost in smoking initiation in adolescent females occured in the late 1960s.In 1967 the tobacco industry launched "niche" brands aimed exclusively at women. The most popular was Virginia Slims. The visuals of this campaign emphasized a woman who was strong, independent and very thin. Consequently and ironically in conjuction with the rise of the women's movement, initiation in female adolescents nearly doubled, from 3.7% between 1964 and 1967 to 6.2 % between 1972 and 1975 (NHIS data). During the same period, rates for adolescent males remained stable.

Thus in four distinct instances over the past 100 years, innovative and directed tobacco marketing campaigns were associated with marked surges in primary demand from adolescents only in the target group. The first two were directed at males and the second two at females. Of course other factors helped to entrench smoking in society, such as the provision of cigarettes during war time and the romanticization of actors smoking in the movies. Yet it is clear from the data that advertising has been an overwhelming force in attracting new users. However despite subsequent regulations barring advertisement geared to minors, the tobacco industry nonetheless has retained its targeted approach.

How can minor purchase cigarette so easily? Although 46 states in USA and Europe have law prohibiting the sale of cigarettes to minors, compliance has been consistently poor in many communities. Furthermore only nine states have stopped the sale of cigarettes in vending machines, and just 22 states prohibit the free distribution of cigarettes to the underage individuals. Many legislators and health officials have suggested that the sale of cigarettes should require licensing similar to that for the sale of alcohol.

The tobacco industry may be relying on a more insidious strategy to gain new customers- that is, through smokeless tobacco. It is estimated that 7.5 million people in the US use tobacco in this way, with snuff (shredded tobacco that is sucked but not chewed) being the most popular. A 1994 wall street journal article reported that tobacco companies doctor their snuff products to increase the nicotine that the mouth can absorb- an alarming assertion, given that the average age of first-time snuff user is nine years. The articles argued that these companies try to appeal to young people with pleasant-testing, milder forms that are lower in free nicotine (that is,in a form immediately available for absorption) and then to graduate these consumers to very potent, very addictive brands high in free nicotine. Although the tobacco companies admit they can control the amount of nicotine in the product, they deny that they do so to addict individuals.

2.5.4 Smoking in Women:

In Asia smoking rates though are generally low but there are some increasing and surprising conceptions. For instance, 67% of women in Andhra Pradesh (India) smoke as against 40% in the rural areas of Thailand. China and Nepal have high rates of smoking (80-90%) but women behave differently. In China smoking in women is very rare indeed whereas in Nepal as many women smoke as do men. whereas smoking against women in the industrialized countries is on the decline, it is increasing in the developing countries. It has been estimated that 20% to 25% of women who smoke are sure to die prematurely of smoking.Amongst women smokers, smoking is responsible for around 40% of heart diseases deaths, 55% of Lethal strokes and among women of all ages, 80% of lung cancer deaths and 30% of all cancer deaths.

Over the last few year, death rate in women from lung cancer have more than doubled in Japan, Norway, Poland, Sweden and UK, and have increased more than 200% in Australia, Denmark and New Zealand and have increased by more than 300% in Canada and the USA(World Health, April-May,1990).

In India smoking in women is equally serious. A survey involving 25800 women in India found 41% of them using tobacco in one form or the other. In rural areas of Goa, 54% Hindu women and 34% Christian women were found to either smoke or chew tobacco (Kanwar and Kanwar,1991).

Smoking affects women's health in many ways specific to them and that puts them at added risk. Women smokers have higher rates of cervical cancer. Women who smoke as well as use contraceptive pills are several times more likely to develop cardiovascular diseases than those who use neither.

Smoking adversely affects women reproductive health and increases significantly the risk of earlier menopause miscarriage, and low birth weight habits. Habitual women cigarette smokers have 21% frequency of infertility *vis a vis* 14% among non smokers and 12% among those who take snuff of chew tobacco (Kanwar and Kanwar,1991). Menstrual disorders appear significantly higher amongst smokers. Smokers as compared to nonsmokers are more likely to have irregular menses especially in their fourth and fifth decades of life.

Cigarette smoke in known to affect gemate viability, fertilisation, early embryonic cleavage, embryo transport and implantation events. It is now established that the smokers have 2.5 to 10% increase in miscarriages compared with the nonsmokers and further this is dose dependent.

Smoking during pregnancy retards fatal growth resulting in low birth weights. Smoking mothers irrespective of their national, racial and socio-economic status and geographical barriers are more likely than non smokers to give birth to underweight babies; the infants of smoking mothers have an average weight of about 200gms less than that of non smokers and a greater percentage of smokers' babies weight less than 2500 gms at birth. Further, babies of the tobacco users have reduced chances of survival. The lower weight of babies amongst smokers cannot be explained as a result of shortened gestational age because the latter is not significantly altered due to smoking. Other causes have to be found. Oxygen deprivation (caused by carbon monoxide) of the fetus is said to be more important reason. Nicotine, in addition to carbon monoxide, may also contribute to smaller size of smokers' babies. Some studies suggest that cigarette smoking depresses women's appetite during pregnancy and this shows up in the underweight and malnourished fetuses.

Complications in pregnancy, pretern delivery and late fetal and new-born deaths are also higher amongst smokers. Further, a number of studies have shown an increase in the incidence of still births, and neonatal and postneonatal deaths amongst the smokers. If current trends of tobacco smoking continues, the global death toll from tobacco by the year 2025 may increase to 8 million deaths per year and a large proportion of these will be women.

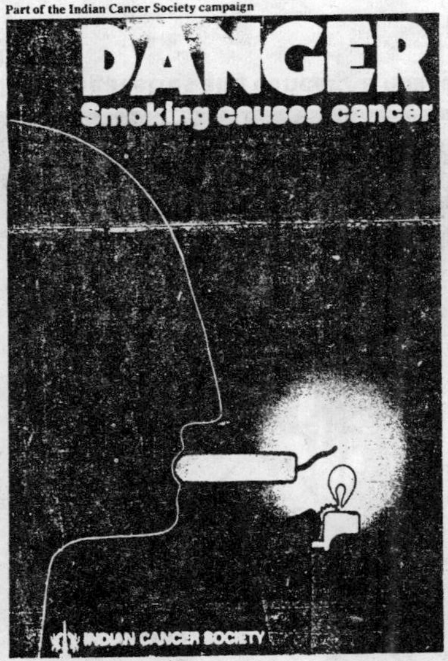

Fig. 3 B

Fig. 3 A

Source: Indian Society on Tobacco and Health
S-281, Panch Shila Park,
New Delhi-110017

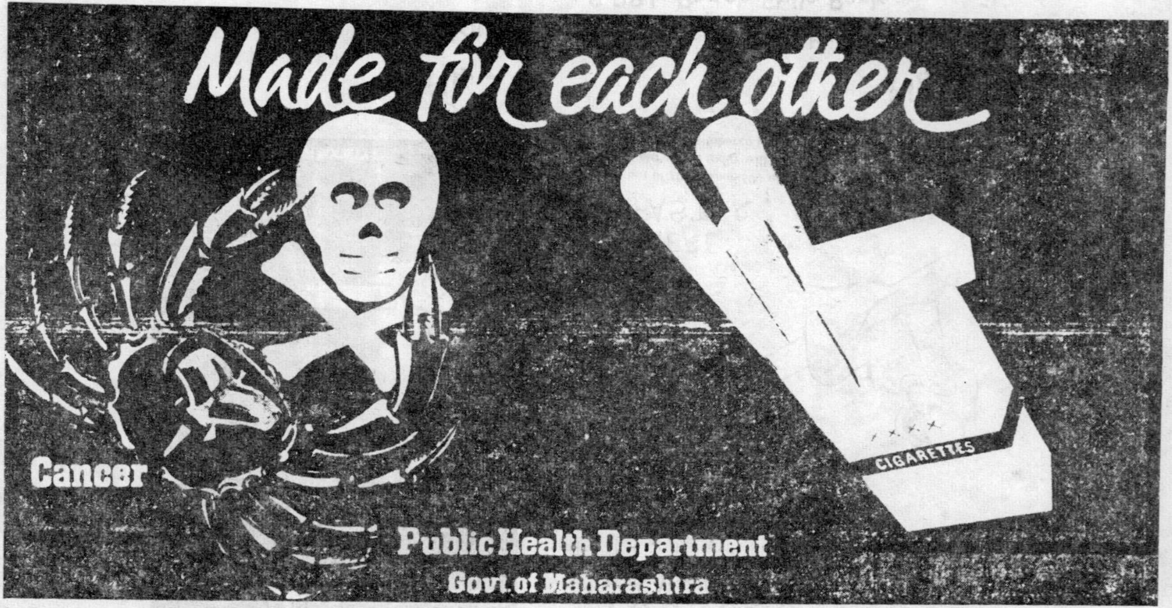

'Made for each other...cigarettes and cancer,' a hoarding launched by the Maharashtra government in its cancer control programme

Fig. 3 C

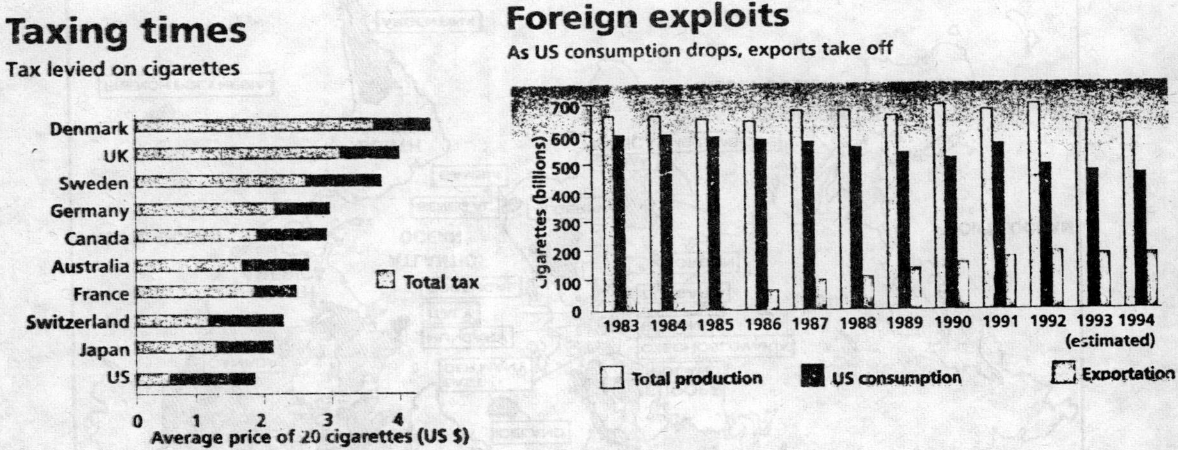

Fig. 4 Source: Scientific American, May, 1995

Where tobacco advertising is banned
GREENLAND
ARCTIC OCEAN
NORWAY
FINLAND
ICELAND
CANADA
EUROPE
EAST GER MANY
POLAND
CZECHOSLOVAKIA
HUNGARY
ROMANIA
ITALY
ASIA
BULGARIA
PORTUGAL
NORTH AMERICA
ATLANTIC OCEAN
JORDON
PACIFIC OCEAN
PACIFIC OCEAN
SENEG AL
ALGERIA
GAMBIA
SUDAN
SOUTH AMERICA
AFRICA
MOZAMBIQUE
SINGAPORE
FRENCH POLYNESIA
INDIAN OCEAN
AUSTRALIA
ARGENTINA

Fig. 5

2.6 Steps to Reduce Smoking

Some of the measures recommended by the antismoking lobby includes:

(1) *Making it mandatory for cigarette and bidi manufacturers to print more specific health warnings on packets,* for example, the current "cigarette smoking is injurious to health" ought to be replaced by an unambiguous "cigarettes cause cancer" or "cigarettes cause heart problems". In India, unlike in most developed countries, it is not mandatory to print on packaging the tar and nicotine content of the product. But given the illiteracy levels, not to speak of the variable vernacular, it remains open to debate how meaningful warning will be in this country. In April 1976 the statutory warning on cigarette packets and advertising came into effect. Yet the governments has not felt the need to extend the warning to zarda and chewing tobacco which account for 75% of the tobacco produced in the country. The cigarette-bidi consumption ratio is 1:13 which should indicate the largeness of the sector that goes uncovered by the statutory warning. However, some NGOS and Governmental Departments are now becoming concious. The warning by Indian Cancer Society and Indian Society on Tobacco and Health is shown on Fig3.

(2) *Increasing the price of tobacco products:* In its effort to dissuade cigarette smoking, the government had hiked excise duty by a whopping 1,133 % over the late ten years. A 10 % increase in cigarette prices reduces consumption by 4% mostly by keeping new smokers away. The drop would probably be much larger in population that are highly sensitive to price hikes, such as teenagers. Because the vast majority of smokers begin in their teens a major drop in teenage society would seriously threaten the future of tobacco industry. The American Heart Association, The American Cancer Society and the America Lung Association have recommended a $2 increase in the federal tax per pack of cigarettes. Their counsel is based in part on data from Canada and California where cigarettes tax hikes have significantly reduced consumption. The potential benefits of high tobacco taxes are many. Several states have earmarked the revenue for public health education campaigns, antitobacco advertising and health care for the poor. The product condition on US consumption and tax levied on cigarettes is shown in Fig4.

(3) *Banning all cigarette advertising* has been contemplated but never put into effect in India because countries like Italy and Poland where advertising is totally prohibited- have reported to discernible drops in consumption (Fig5). Interestingly, banning of advertisement alone reduced cigarette consumption by 11.3% in New Zealand, 11% in Canada and 10% in Norway.

(4) It is time that the *anti tobacco legislation is introduced in Parliament* failing which the judiciary may in all likehood

have to direct the centre to adopt proper legislation while simultaneously recommendation early rehabilitation of the growers, workers, traders and vendors. In fact the government has been having second thoughts on the anti tobacco legislation because the centre does not know how to rehabilitate 75 lakh bidi workers and 60 lakh tobacco growers, if tobacco agriculture is banned. Hence, steps must be taken to engage these people in some other work before taking a decision. Government subsidies should be given for conversion of tobacco corps to other plants.

(5) *Removal of harmful substances from tobacco smoke* by filtering the smoke or by manufacturing filter tipped cigarettes may be another preventive measure. Modification of tobacco can also be done. Some strains of tobacco plants can have very low nicotine content. Tar and carcinogen content of tobacco smoke can be reduced by various methods of treatment of tobacco. Regulations should be introduced whereby purchaser of any brand of tobacco products can discover the average amounts of carcinogens. Moreover, there must be strict regulations for export. For example, actually, there are no US imposed regulations on the labelling, Tar content or advertisements of tobacco products exported to other nations.

(6) *Anti smoking clinics should be opened throughout the world.* Smokers can get expert advice from those who have succeeded in freeing themselves from the addictions of tobacco. Such clinics have been started in Sweden with great

success. The clinics can also give free clinical trails and counselling to smokers to free them from this dreadful addiction.

(7) *Prohibition of sale of tobacco products to children and minors.* It is important that law be issued by the government to ban sale of cigarettes to persons below the age of 18. From the standpoint of public health it is very clear that a battle plant must emphasise intervention of programmes that specially target children and adolescents. As the motto of World Health Organization is "health for All" in 21st century, the future citizens must by prevented from damaging their health by smoking and taking tobacco products.

(8) *Restriction on workplace and public smoking should be imposed on.* The concerned citizens, public health officials, government representatives and health care providers must join forces to adopt disciplinary actions if necessary in this matter. In fact, in Delhi, the prohibition of smoking and nonsmokers health protection bill was introduced in the Assembly on August,7 1995. Recently the Delhi High Court has issued orders to both the Union and the Delhi Government to ban smoking in public places. The bill known as "Delhi Prohibition of Smoking and Nonsmokers Health Protection Bill" disallows smoking in public places, bans selling of cigarettes, bidis and cigars to those below the age of 18 years and also within a radius of 100 m around education". The bill envisages a penalty of Rs.100/- for the first offence followed by Rs.500/- for subsequent offences. It also bans advertise-

ments for propagating smoking and sponsorship of tobacco products during a cultural or sports events. The violators of this provision would have to pay a fine of Rs.500-1000 besides serving a 3 month prison sentence. The West Bengal government has also put a ban on public smoking and have levied 10% luxury tax to push down the sale of cigarettes. (see section 2.5.1)

2.7 How to Quit

The American Cancer Society suggests two possible "recipes" for breaking the smoking habit. Of course, trying the suggestions from one list does not rule out those from the other list.

Recipe A

1. Decide to smoke only once a hour, or decide to stop smoking for an entire hour and the start lengthening that time by half hour.

2. Make it hard to get at a cigarette. Wrap up the package and put elastic bands around it. Smoke with your left hand if you usually smoke with your right hand.

3. Switch to a brand you do not like. Buy only one pack at a time.

4. If you always have a smoke with your coffee, switch to tea or fruit juice.

5. Do something for your body. Get back in shape, exercise is great for relation.

6. Call up your friends and tell them you are going to quit.

7. If you quit for one day, you can quit for another. Try it.

8. Save all the money you would have spent on cigarette and by yourself something. You deserve it.

9. If you break down and have a cigarette, don't worry. Some people have several tries before they at last succeed.

Recipe B

1. Cut out a cigarette a day.

2. Make each cigarette a special decision- and put of making the decision.

3. Don't give up cigarettes completely. Carry one around with you in case of need. You will find in the end you are saving it- permanently.

4. Don't quit forever. Just stop for a day and tomorrow try it for another day and tomorrow and tomorrow and tomorrow.

5. Tell your friends and family you are quitting. A public commitment bolsters will power.

6. Pick a day- the day you quit. And quit.

7. Hide all evidences of cigarettes. Ashtray and matches, so you are not reminded of the habit.

8. Lay in a supple of chewing gum, cough, sweets or peanuts to nibble instead of reaching for a smoke.

(Source: World Health)

Give up smoking

Abstaining from cigarettes completely is better than cutting down a little at a time, a process that stretches our agonies of withdrawl, report Saul Schiffman and Dr. Murray Jarvik of the University of California at Los Angeles School of Medicine, in an American Cancer Society Journal on world smoking and health. The most acute withdrawl problem identified by about 90% of the exsmokers in the study, comes in the first two weeks and hits hardest around 7 P.M. The craving is so powerful that among the partly abstinent smokers it induces relapse and virtually ensures failure of further efforts to give up smoking. But among those who give it up all at once, there is an easing of withdrawl symptoms in the first few days, and this makes it easier to hold out until withdrawl troubles run their course.

How can you help

* Stop tobacco smoking, chewing and eating. If use of tobacco is stopped, risk of death among smokers declines to that of non users of tobacco in 10 years time.

* Set a good example yourself- be a non-smoker.

* Be a good parent and stop smoking in your house, for the sake of your own health and that of your family, and prevent your children acquiring the smoking habit.

* Be a good teacher and friend and set a good example to other.

* Stop smoking during pregnancy.

* Join the antismoking-chewing campaign.

1. To prevail upon the government to have ban on advertisement in T.V., Radio, newspapers, magazines, handbills, posters, hoardings, wrappers and sales promotion activities of every type sponsorship of games, beauty contests etc.,

2. To prohibit by Legislation smoking in all public places-Government offices, aeroplanes, railways, public transport, cinemas, schools, colleges, hospitals, courts, police stations etc. etc...

3. To conduct health education program for all especially the students and staff of schools and colleges through public information and public education. Radio, TV print and newspapers, puppet shows, cinemas, cartoons and lectures.

4. Pleading for potent compulsory health warnings on cigarettes, cigarette packets, bidis and bidi packets, pan masalas and other tobacco products, and on their advertisements.

5. Campaigning for banning of sale of tobacco in any form such as cigarettes, bidis, pan masala, which should be allowed to be sold in Governments shops like in the case of liquor. Not to sell to minors.

6. Helping non smokers who are in majority and helping them to fight for their Rights and not to let anyone smoke near them. Non smokers to be bold but courteous.

CHAPTER 3

NEWS FROM RESEARCH WORLD

Speedy Recovery up in Smoke

cigarettes smokers can expect extra-long stays in the recovery room after surgery, according to an analysis of 327 surgical patient's charts at the Monmouth Medical Centre in New Jersey. Only 7% of non smokers stayed more than two hours in recovery, versus 19% of smokers. And 38% of non-smokers stayed less than an hour, versus 23% of smokers.

Controversely, some factors traditionally believed to affect recovery including the type of surgery, type of anaesthesia, age and obesity-played only a minor role, according to Dr. David Handling, the anestheosiologist who conducted the study. He said smokers' respiratory reflexes may return less quickly, and they may be more prone to very low or very high blood pressure.

Killer Cigarettes

The message of the new US Surgeon Generals' report on the health hazards of smoking is even grimmer than the report from the same office 15 years ago. The evidence is much stronger that cigarette smoking is implicated in heart disease and cancer, and new data now link it to many more bronchial diseases, allergies and adverse reaction to drugs. Cigarettes pose particular risks to pregnant women, children and workers exposed to toxic chemicals. Summing it all up, US Health, Education and Welfare Secretary concludes that "Smoking is even more dangerous indeed far more than dangerous-than was supposed in 1964".

That conclusion will surprise virtually no one. Most smokers themselves are well aware of the danger. Most have either tried to stop or would like to. The problem remains; how to break the tobacco habit?

Smoke(less) Signals

Chewing tobacco and snuff, the so-called smokeless tobacco many American young people are beginning to use, may cause mouth and throat cancer, according to the New England Journal of Medicine. The warning is based on a report from Central North Carolina- where 30% of the women "dip" snuff regularly-indicating that mouth and throat cancer rates among these women range from 4 to nearly 50 times the national norm.

The problem has long been common in countries like India, China and Thailand, where snuff and chewing tobacco are traditionally popular, and oral-cancer death rates among the world"s highest.

"Puffed" up cholesterol

Here is some news that might make smokers finally decide to quit. Several studies involving about 50,000 people found that a person's cholesterol level is directly associated with the number of cigarettes smoked per day.

Each cigarette raises total cholesterol an average of half a point according to researchers at the Amercian Health Foundation. For example, among men and premenopausal women, those who smoked 30 cigarettes a day had cholesterol levels 15 points higher than non-smokers did. Elevated cholesterol increases the risk of heart attack.

Precisely how cigarettes affect cholesterol levels in unclear, but Dr. Randall Harris of the foundation speculates that smoking may change levels of sex hormones, or that smokers may consume diets higher in fat than non-smokers do. Both factors could heighten levels of serum cholesterol. The good news is that the ex-smokers in the studies had the same cholesterol levels as those who had never smoked.

Smoke Gets in their Ears

A study in the Journal of the Amercian Medical Association suggests that cigarette smoking may be harmful to child's ears. Dr. Michael Kraemer and co-workers at Seattle's Children's Orthopaedic Hospital and Medical Centre compared two groups of children undergoing surgery-one for a chronic ear diseases (persistent fluid in the middle ear) and one for the ailments. They found that the ear diseases group more often had a history of recurrent ear infection, nasal congestion, allergies- and household cigarette smoke exposure. Ear-diseases risk increased when adults in the home smoked more than three packs a day.

Smoking and Pregnancy

Premature separation of the placenta from the uterus wall-called placental abruption- raises the risk that the baby will die or be born prematurely. Now a team headed by pathologist Richard Naeye of Pennsylvania State University College of Medicine has found that smoking during pregnancy is strongly related to one type of fatal abruption.

In a study of 4,570 pregnancies, the team found that the death rate from this type of abruption was 3.3 per thousand babies of non-smokers. The rates increased to 4.7 per thousand when the mothers had smoked one to ten cigarettes per day while pregnant, and rose to 5.2 per thousand when they had smoked 11 to 20 cigarettes a day. Dr. Naeye advises women, who want to be safe, not to smoke during pregnancy.

Earlier Menopause with Smoking

Women who smoke are likely to undergo menopause at a younger age than non-smokers, according to the findings of the two studies, involving more than 3,500 middle-aged women, published in The Lancet, a British medical journal. In one of the studies women at ages 48 to 49 who smoked a pack or more a day (heavy smokers) were nearly twice as likely to be past menopause as a women who had never smoked. And the more a women smokes, the earlier her menopause tends to occur. For example heavy smokers were more likely to be past menopause than light smokers (half a pack a day or less).

This "striking association" between smoking and the onset of menopause was accidentally discovered while Dr. Hershel Jick, Jane porter and Dr. Alan Morrison of the Boston Collaborative Drug Surveillance Program, a continuing international project, exploring the links between smoking and heart diseases. (Smoking is known to increase a person's chances of developing heart diseases, and one study indicates that women past menopause have a higher rate of coronary diseases than pre-menopausal women of the same age). A closer look at the data suggested that smoking might actually precipitate early menopause. This itself may be the real explanation for the apparent association previously found between menopause and heart disease.

Tobacco Wars

Non-smokers have been fighting for years to get smoking banned from public places. They argue that the habit subjects non-smokers to unpleasant odours and eye irritation. Smokers have countered that as long as they are not hurting anyone except themselves they have the right to do so as please. That reply has now been undermined by researchers at the University of California at San Diego who found that long-term exposure to cigarette smoke causes measurable lung damage in people who do not smoke.

The study, reported in the New England Journal of Medicine by exercise physiologist James White and Dr. Herman Froeb, examined the effects of smoking on 2,100 men and women. Within this group; non-smokers who did not work in smoky environments came out best on tests on the lungs' capacity to inhale and exhale air. Those who had smoked more than 40 cigarettes a day for more than 20 years had the worst results.

Carrots May Prevent Head and Neck Cancers

Cigarettes, chewing tobacco and alcohol are major risk factors for head and neck cancers, but new reseach suggests that men and women alike should consider replacing the dangling cigarette with the beta-carotene-rich carrot. Beta carotene which the body converts to Vitamin A, may reverse a pre-cancerous condition called leukoplakia, which appears as whitish parches in the mouth and throat. Previous studies have shown that Vitamin A can reverse leukoplakia but can also be toxic at the levels required to do its work. In a pilot study reported last year by Dr. Harminder Garewal of the University of Arizona Cancer Centre in Tucson, 25 patients with leukoplakia took 30 milligrams of beta carotene a day, roughly equal to eating four to six carrots. The whitish patches decreased or disappeared in more than 70% of the subjects as long as they continued taking beta carotene. There were none of the toxic side effects associated with Vitamin A supplements.

Garewal says a larger trial may show that an inexpensive betacarotene supplement could serve an important public health role. Head and neck cancers are serious problems worldwide, especially where good nutrition and proper mouth care are lacking. Prevention is important because surgical treatment can leave patients seriously disfigured and unable to speak or hear normally.

Smoking more and Remembering Less

Perhaps cigarette packets should carry an important caution: "Smoking may make you stupid".

A team of researchers at the University of California in Los Angeles (UCLA) reported in the American Journal of Psychiatry that the nicotine in cigarette smoke may cause a reduction in a person's ability to learn and remember. Of 23 habitual smokers, 12 were given cigarettes containing no nicotine, and 11 smoked cigarettes containing a specific amount of nicotine.

Subjects in both groups were then asked to recall as many words as they could from a 75-word list. To test organizational skills, the words were drawn from a number of categories (professions, animals, names), but arranged in random order. The subjects were graded not only on the total number of words recalled, but also on how many they remembered by category. In a pre-smoking trial the groups were equivalent. But in the trials which followed, the non-nicotine group was able to remember significantly more words than the nicotine group.

REFERENCES

*Alkondon M, Pereira ESR and Albuquerque EX .. *J Pharmacol Expther* (In press).

*Balasubramanium T, *Science Reporter*, **19** (80), 472, 1982.

*Benowitz NL and Jacob P, ***Methods Cli PharmacolTher.***, **86**, 483, 1994.

*Benowitz NL and Henningfield JE , *New Eng J Med*, **331**, 123, 1994.

*Bhide SV and Pratap Al., *Food Cosmet Toxicol.*, **19**, 481, 1981.

Castleden CM, *Brit Med. J.* **4** (5947), 736, 1974.

*Clarke PBS, *Ciba Fnd symp.*, **152**, 152 1990.

*Cortan RS, Kumar V and Robbins RL., Pathogenic Basis of Diseases, pub. by WB Saunders co, USA pg.469, 1989.

*Dusek DE and Girdano DA, Drugs; a factual account, Pub. by Newbery Awards records inc. NY. pg. 141, 1987.

*Frankenhaeuser M et al, *Psyhcopharmacologia*, **13**, 311, 1971.

*Freeman FS, Theory and pratice of psychological testing, pub. by Oxford & IBH pub. co. New Delhi, pg. 247, 1976.

*Goodman Gilman A, The Pharmacological Basis of Therapeutics, 9th edition, pub. by Mcgrawhill, USA, 1996

*Gray R, Rajan AS, Radcliffe KA, Yakehiro M and Dani JA, *Nature,* **383**, 713, 1996.

*Gupta S and Gupta BK., *Ind J Chest Dis Allied Sci.*, **28**, 183, 1986.

*Heimer I, Zahon DS, Churchill L, Kalivas PW and Wohltmann G., *Neuroscience,* **41**, 89, 1991.

*Hoffman D, Sanghvi LD and Wynder EL., *Ind J Cancer,* **14**, 49, 1974.

*Holbrook JH, Harrisons principles of internal medicine, pub. By. Mcgrawhill Co. NY pg. 855, 1987.

*Imperato A, Mulas A and Dichiara G., *Eur J Pharmacol,* **132**, 337, 1989.

*Kanwar KC and Kanwar U., *Everyman's Science,* 1991

*Keith CH and Tesh PG, *Tob Sci,* **9**, 61, 1965.

*Levin ED et al, *Psychopharmacology.*, **123**, 55, 1992.

*Murdia US and Mehta FJ., *Food Cehm Toxicol*, **20**, 269, 1982.

*Oborne DJ, *Ergonomics*, **26**, 1163, 1983.

*Pakhale SS, Jayant K and Bhide SV, *Ind J Chest dis Allied Sci,* **32**, 75, 1990.

*Pontieri FF et al, *Neuroreport*, **5**, 2561, 1994.

*Pontieri FF et al, Proc Nath Acad Sci, 92, 12304, 1995.

*Pontieri FF, Tanda G, Orzi F and Dichiara G., *Nature*, **382**, 255, 1996.

*Sandberg PR and Levin T. *Pharmacol Ther.* (in press), 1996

*Self DN, Barnhart WJ, Lehman DA and Nestler EJ, *Science*, **271**, 1586, 1996.

*Squire LR and Lindlamb E,The biology of memory, Pub. By. Schattauer Suttgart, 1990.

*Sharma PVR, Dhand R, Malhotra A, Malhotra S, Sharma BK, *Ind J Chest Dis Allied Sci.*, **32**, 83, 1990.

*Srinivas Kumar D, *Maffers MIT pune Journal IIT*, **11**,10,1994.

*Stolerman IP anad Jarvis MJ, *Psychopharmacology*, **117**, 2, 1995.

*Sundararaj DD and Thulasidas G, Botany of field crops, Pub. By. Macmillan India ltd., 1993.

*Surgeon General report, Office on smoking and health, United States Dept. Health and Human Services, the health consequences of smoking, nicotine addiction, Government printing office,Washington DC, 1988.

*Swaroop V and Agnihotri MS., *J Ind Med, Ass.*, **96**, 30,80, 1998.

*Thomas GA et al, *New Engl, J Med.*, **332**, 988, 1995.

*Westman EC, Levin ED and Rose JE, *Arch Intern Med*, **153**, 1917, 1993.

*Wilson JD, Braunwalld E, lasselbacher KJ, Harrison principles of internal medicine, Pub. By. Mcgrawhill inc, NY 2, 2158, 1991.

*Whiting P and Lindstrom *J., Proc Natn Acad Sci.*, USA, **4**, 595, 1987.

*WHO Tech Rep *Ser.* 695, 7, 1983.

*WHO Cron, **36**, 156, 1982.